LOOKING
for that
CITY

LOOKING
for that
CITY

Moving from Darkness into His Light

PAUL E. MYERS

Outskirts Press, Inc.
Denver, Colorado

Looking For That City
Moving From Darkness Into His Light
All Rights Reserved.
Copyright © 2010 Paul E. Myers
v3.0

Cover Photo © 2010 JupiterImages Corporation. All rights reserved - used with permission.

Outskirts Press, Inc.
http://www.outskirtspress.com

ISBN: 978-1-4327-4880-7

Outskirts Press and the "OP" logo are trademarks belonging to Outskirts Press, Inc.

PRINTED IN THE UNITED STATES OF AMERICA

To the memory of
Marjorie Pietsch Myers, my mother,
and
in honor of
Deanna Tully Myers, my wife, and
Michelle Myers Kish, my daughter.

Each one is a testimony of Strength,
and an exemplar of Grace.

I am, indeed, thankful.

ACKNOWLEDGEMENTS

God's working in my life has been through many precious people. I would not have accomplished this writing without the experiences and influences of these loved ones.

Neale Pryor, Mark Tully and Ben Myers; three men who built within me the belief I could move from darkness into the light.

Sarah Minnis; as a professional career coach and a special friend, she encouraged my public speaking, from which this book was born.

Bill Sirdovsky; who couldn't know what he started by saying, "Paul, you ought to write a book."

Virgil Hammontree and Jim Welch; I value their insightful critiques and their friendships.

I am thankful for the many Christians who have been used by God through the years to influence my life. In so many ways – to cry when crying was helpful, to pray because praying is always helpful, and to laugh, proving it can be helpful, too.

And, my wife, Deanna Tully Myers; I am truly a blessed man through God's extraordinary gift of her in this life. Her constant devotion to God and to me has sustained, nurtured and enriched my life.

TABLE OF CONTENTS

Introduction 1

ONE   Higher Ground.. 5

TWO   Unto A New Song...................................... 15

THREE   A Few Skipped Beats 27

FOUR   A New Mind 41

FIVE   Giving Voice.. 69

SIX   Vested In Truth 91

SEVEN   What Must I Do?..................................... 109

EIGHT   Mighty Or Real?...................................... 125

NINE   Stepping Stones 139

TEN   So, What Now?....................................... 159

Epilogue 179

INTRODUCTION

LOOKING FOR THAT CITY

A life without introspection is a life without a course. A life with too much introspection never pursues its course. Many, including me, too often live in the extremes, not knowing the course, or not pursuing the course. We miss the balance which yields a blessed life.

What transpires in one's life to restrain movement towards a blessed life? Why would one stagnate even when the course is known? Why would a soldier only march in place, struggling against stepping out in full stride? Why would I, as a Christian called to be a soldier of the cross, find myself marking time and rarely marching onward?

My walk through many realms of my life has largely been a story of marking time. Recalling my years in the high school, marching band, I could play the music, I could know the drills, I could wear the uniform, but what if I never stepped out in formation? I would have been useless to the band. Similarly, in my Christian walk, I could know the Word, I could know the purpose, I could clothe myself in Christ, but until I decided to step out with Him, I was useless for God's purposes.

Far more than understanding what restrains one, the real blessings of introspection come from what transpires to spur change in a person seemingly stuck in place. The causes are many; sometimes inspirational, sometimes tragic. For me, the causes led to stepping out of mediocrity by learning how to step out of depression's deep, cold vacuum. One of the steps was trusting "in all things the Spirit works for the good of those who love Him, who have been called according to His purpose" (Romans 8:28). Ultimately, for His glory and purpose, God in His working and timing, can create a soul-felt yearning to reach a higher plane in one's life, love, and service to Him.

By His working through triumphs and tragedies, joys and sorrows, and through mental illness, I gained the will to press onward. I found, or more accurately, God worked in me the desire to reach a higher plane. I began looking for that city, Heaven, as a means of drawing closer to, and drawing power from God.

I have long been involved in the Lord's church, but largely was marking time, seldom stepping upward to new planes of love or service. In seeking higher ground, I purposed to step out of old, settled ways. I forced myself to start speaking out for God, beginning with short devotionals. While for decades I submitted to a sinful fear, always keeping silent, it was a very rich blessing to find my voice for Him.

While still living in emotional turmoil, in the first few talks a theme of looking towards the prize of Heaven emerged. From this theme, my course out of mental illness also emerged. Each tentative step set my vision higher, set my hopes higher, and brought me out of my darkness and into His light.

I first envisioned this book as a collection of meditations about the promised glories of Heaven. However, the single focus became saccharin. Certainly, Heaven will be so sweet, but there is more to the journey than only seeking the promised victory at the end of this life. Where is the real victory without the overcoming of trials? The celebration of victory is brighter for having through Christ overcome the darkness.

The glorious plan of salvation and the story of one's salvation are made brighter because redemption is from the depths of sin, tragedy, and darkness. Redemption is not pursued as one who knows no sin, but as one who truly needs Jesus' all-sufficiency to lift His own from spiritually, shifting sands to solid, higher ground.

It is troubling to see so many people, including those within the Lord's church, who are struggling within emotional illnesses. They are bogged down in spirit-killing, mental quicksand, unable to find sure footing on solid, victorious, spiritual ground. Some are facing transient, situational darkness. Others are fighting to overcome harsh, deeply-rooted imbalances. In either case, each one must overcome the extreme thoughts and emotions which constrain them in darkness. As I have found, I hope to convey this assurance - whatever the trial, it can be borne. Whatever the darkness, the true light of Jesus will banish it. We can both find our course, and pursue our course.

This is a memoir, but there is no value in its telling unless the promises of God are affirmed. I have not written to celebrate my past darkness, but to celebrate the healing process of moving from my darkness into God's Light. I joyfully share how I have been changed according to the certain promises of His Word. The Spirit's working in my renewal was not through a unique outpouring of God's grace. It was not through a never-before-fathomed mystery. God's sure provision was delivered just as He promised – through the steadfastness of His Word, the surety of His grace, and through the love of His people fulfilling their calling according to His will.

While pursuing higher ground, I learned more was necessary than simply reaching a new plane and staking a claim. I had to grow in the preparation to defend the claim, holding fast to the gain. Like soldiers who take a hill in battle, once it is theirs they must defend it. In my case, it was climbing out of the valleys of depression, but knowing challenges to my renewed mind are sure to come. I can celebrate the gain while learning the tools to defend the higher ground. Thus, this pursuit is about drawing closer to God, while purposing my life towards Heaven. Through Christ's strength I will stake my claim every step of the way.

I have not sought to define a step-by-step plan because I am confident God, and the Spirit working through His Word, will chart each one's course out of darkness, specific to your darkness. God had to show me each step, for many I could not foresee. And, from my steps I pray that others will find their first step to move from darkness into His Light.

By His course set for me, I came to know truly who I am. I had to acknowledge my sins, seek Him as the source of renewal, and trust the promises which I so long had doubted. I developed a two-way conversation with God through His Word and prayer. Most of all, I had to relinquish control of my life to Him. Not a single step was easy, but every step was crucial.

While learning to speak out, I relied on the words of hymns, as I also have in these pages. Yet, I know that our songs, while inspirational, are not the inspired words of God. Of their own merit, they cannot hold up as Truth, for they are inspired from the hearts of man. Our songs may be our sincerest voice to God, and the language we depend upon for praise, for solace, and for hope. But, above all, we must rely upon God's inspired Word.

God has blessed me richly through spiritual songs. When my pursuit of both prayer and Bible study were severely lacking, hymns were the language connecting me to God; the tether which kept me from falling away. In times of depression when I didn't know what to pray, I'd sing, "I need Thee every hour, most gracious Lord; no tender voice like Thine can peace afford." In seeking to step out for the Lord, my words in song were, "I'm pressing on the upward way, new heights I'm gaining every day." In times of trial; "I'll not be moved, I'll not be moved from Mount Zion. My faith is anchored there and it shall stand." And, in contented times, I cherish singing, "When peace like a river attendeth my way, it is well, it is well with my soul." I am convinced that God used my lifelong love of singing as a means to renew my mind, and to establish His purposes in me.

As I seek an ever-higher plane of devotion to God, I cast my gaze towards Heaven, but also to a higher understanding of what He has brought me from, of how He works in my life, and of what is needful to live in the full assurance of His Light. Add it all together; it was God's way to move me from marking time to marching onward!

All my praise is to Him!

ONE

HIGHER GROUND

How could I have known the powerful memories born within the walls of a simple, white church building? Not until fifty years later would I know the blessings sown into my life as a quiet, cotton-top, country kid. Now, I often wonder if those who richly touched my life have any idea of their effect.

It seems the days in Arcadia, Texas, in the late 1950's, advanced in a predictable rhythm and order. Much of the order was established by Saturdays and Sundays. Saturdays always included laying out clothes, and polishing shoes for Sunday. "Sunday" was synonymous with "church," and church was the securing rhythm and order of life.

There was security in sensing the importance of the rhythm; the beats always sure. Sure enough, even when we didn't have a car because Dad needed it for work, Mom dressed up my brothers and me, and we walked to church. My polished shoes lost their luster by the time we got there, but it didn't matter – just a quick swipe down the back of my pant legs and all was well.

Aside from the verdant, Jordan River scene behind the baptistery, little distinguished the church from any other meeting place. There was nothing 'high church' about its appearance; just an honest place which depended upon the people inside to make it a church. It sat next to the old, dilapidated Cargile's Drug Store which, ironically, didn't sell drugs any longer; just comics, candy, and Cokes. A half-block in one direction stood the Quonset-style fire station. A half-block in the other direction sat a beer joint wedged between the highway and the railroad tracks. Schultz's pink stucco, grocery store, the green and white Texaco station, and the feed store pretty much completed the center of town. The church made up the center of life, though I was years from knowing how central it was.

The young preacher's wife, Mrs. Holland, couldn't know her influence as she played the piano. I loved the sound of it, and watching her play fascinated me. Often, while she played at the close of services, I'd walk next to the piano to watch and listen. She'd see me coming, smile, and make an exaggerated gesture of sliding over on the bench, inviting me to sit with her. I never missed the chance to climb up on the bench. In those moments the love of singing was planted in me.

Years later, it was Mrs. Holland who encouraged a nervous, pimple-faced teenager to sing, though usually I was too scared to even speak. The song sought, "Fill my cup, Lord; come and quench this thirsting of my soul," and foretold a lifelong need. That Sunday the love of songs was nurtured in me. And, not many years later, I led the singing in a huge, mighty fortress of a church in Galveston. Though still scared, yet again, the love of singing grew in me.

How could I have foreseen the memories of walking to church, sitting on the piano bench, and singing those songs would sound a sustained, major chord in my life? Moreover, I could not see that someday the songs would help to save my life; not only my soul, but this earthly life as well.

As a grandfather I'm continually fascinated with the words of little children; the way they can clearly see the world around them. Their words are captivating because they are expressing insights without all the filters we adopt through the years. Though I can't recall my own words at that age, I do recall knowing the predictable rhythm and order of life was going to skip a few beats along the way.

Twenty years later I knew full well, the dreams planted in the fertile soil of youth sometimes don't grow as envisioned. Oh, some bloom splendidly; others are coarse, tenacious weeds. The weeds, fertilized by tragedies, emotional illnesses and sins, are the devil to uproot!

Johnson Oatman was a lay minister and writer of hundreds a hymns in the late 1800's, including *Higher Ground*. He couldn't have known his words so many years later could help change a life. He penned a hymn of confident hope in the Lord. His words express the fervent expectation that a dependence upon the working of the Lord will lift one up to new heights, above doubts and fears, and ultimately to a heavenly plane.

> *I'm pressing on the upward way,*
> *New heights I'm gaining everyday;*
> *Still praying as I onward bound,*
> *"Lord plant my feet on higher ground."*
>
> *My heart has no desire to stay*
> *Where doubts arise and fears dismay;*
> *Tho' some may dwell where these abound,*
> *My prayer, my aim is higher ground.*
>
> *I want to live above the world,*
> *Tho' Satan's darts at me are hurled;*
> *For faith has caught the joyful sound,*
> *The song of saints on higher ground.*
>
> *I want to scale the utmost height,*
> *And catch a gleam of glory bright;*
> *But still I'll pray till Heaven I've found;*
> *"Lord, lead me on to higher ground."*
>
> *Lord, lift me up and let me stand,*
> *By faith on Heaven's table land,*
> *A higher plane than I have found;*
> *Lord, plant my feet on higher ground.*

Now, in middle age, I purposed to move beyond so many issues which restrained me; just existing in the faith, too seldom thriving. There finally had to be some movement in my life towards the resolution of anxieties too long held. What could be done to settle the past so I would be capable of setting a purpose for the future? What could

I do to reconcile the person I claim to be with the person I am? And, could there finally be a persistent light to overwhelm the cold, dark vacuum of depression?

The danger, spiritually, of not answering those questions is a life lived in mediocrity. And, living a life without reconciliation is double-dealing with God; a duplicity of wills, not wholly of God, or of the world. The average of the two is mediocrity. The biblical word is "lukewarm," and the Jesus minces no words about it. "I know your deeds, that you are neither cold nor hot. I wish that you were either one or the other! So, because you are lukewarm – neither hot or cold – I am about to spit you out of my mouth" (Revelation 3:16). Through my exasperation of wounded, fearful living, I adopted the words of *Higher Ground* as stepping stones towards my pursuit beyond mediocrity.

Motivational gurus stress defining a goal and daily holding the goal in sight is critical. My convictions include a dependence upon the Lord, and the equation of my darkness must factor in sin. Integrity before God requires His will to be held up as the goal. *Higher Ground* became my voicing of the goal.

Often, the simplest words can define the goal, and be the first step towards a higher plane. Such words were heard in a sermon by Neale Pryor, a few years ago, just as my wife and I were coming out of a very tragic decade within our family.

Neale, though sadly now burdened by Alzheimer's, was then an intriguing blend of a wise, gentle grandpa mixed with the eye-twinkling mischief of a kid. He held the confident aura derived from a lifelong devotion to God, fused with the warmth of a treasured friend. Listening to him was akin to an afternoon of sitting on the porch with my soft-spoken grandpa sharing old, family stories. When God, through Neale, spoke a message of confident hope in the promised glories of Heaven, the simple phrase, "failure is not final," became a rich assurance of God's grace, which quickened my faltering spirit.

From the hymn's inspiration, and an assurance of hope, I developed the habit of starting everyday with the simple tune, "I'm pressing on the upward way, new heights I'm gaining every day." It became a clear motivation for the day; a context for everything I hope to think, say, and do – pressing on to greater heights with the Lord every day.

Isn't this what God wants from us? As we strive to do His will, isn't this what He asks – for us to love Him just a little bit more today? He asks us to serve Him just a little bit more today, to glorify Him and to reflect His glory just a little bit more today – to become more like Christ every day. The desire to love, serve, and imitate Christ, is the essence of the Apostle Paul's resolve to "strain ahead, to press on, to win the prize for which we have been called, heavenward, in Christ Jesus" (Philippians 3:14).

Paul manifested the mindset of seeking and claiming higher ground. Even while constrained in chains, he exulted with words of joy in his assurance of triumph. While imprisoned, his brothers in the Lord stepped up to speak the Word of God more courageously and fervently. Thus, the cause of Christ was raised higher, and Paul's spirit was lifted higher by his rejoicing in Christ's gain.

As I am writing, another Paul, my son, is in prison. His is a story of one who failed in the matters of which the Apostle Paul warned in I Thessalonians 4:3-7. "It is God's will that you should avoid sexual immorality; that each of you should learn to control his own body in a way that is holy and honorable, not in passionate lust like the heathen, who does not know God…for God did not call us to be impure, but to live a holy life."

This young man was, and is, in many ways a very good man, with many endearing qualities – giving, sensitive, and despite his failings, carries a keen sense of right and wrong. He tried hard to live a Christian life, but tragically he tried to live it by his own power; never submitting every aspect of his life to the power of God. So, he lived his life just one temptation, one sin, and one crisis of judgment away from the failures which continue to bear grievous consequences.

It's been a foreboding journey, through grief and guilt and grinding shame. Now, after all which has been said, and all which has been done for him, there is one message I give him at every opportunity. Failure in not final! By God's grace through Christ's redemption, failure is not final.

My son's mistakes are those which people, both inside and

outside the church, consider "big sins." Though any sin is abhorrent to God, we tend to falsely rank misdeeds; believing others' sins are wretched and our "little" sins are, "oh, not so bad, compared to *that*." Perhaps, the most dangerous transgressions are those we call "secret sins" – the temptations, thoughts, and hidden wrongs which have not been subjected to the cleansing of Christ. Big sins, or little sins, or secret sins, all are failures before God. But, the failure does not have to be final. There is, through Jesus, the complete cure for our double-dealing ways.

Considering failure in a lighter vein, it reminds me of a Kenny Rogers' song about a little boy learning to hit a baseball. I can picture this scene because I tried to learn the same way.

The little boy is trying to hit the ball by tossing it up and swinging as it comes down. On his first pitch, the ball goes up, the ball comes down, and he swings his bat as the ball hits the ground. The second pitch is hardly different from the first – the ball goes up, the ball comes down, again he swings his bat as the ball hits the ground. Listening to the song, you suppose on the next pitch, the little boy is going to connect; he's going to send the ball soaring! Picture him digging in, adjusting his cap, and propping the bat on his shoulder. He makes the pitch; the ball goes up, the ball comes down, the little boy swings all the way around, as the ball hits the ground.

Listening, your heart sinks just as quickly as the ball hitting the ground. You know this was strike three. The little boy has struck out. We think the youngster has failed. But, no, even the boy knows so much better. He picks up the ball, undeterred and with a heart full of optimism. If you've heard the song you'll remember his words, "I never knew I could pitch *that* good!"

He knows, "failure is not final." He'll press on until he learns how to hit, or maybe he'll learn that his "higher ground" is on the pitcher's mound. Whichever, he will press on past his failure. We can press on past our failures, too. Big sins, little sins, or secret sins, our failures are not final. But, Jesus' forgiveness is final! In Him, the old failures are forgotten, and every day begins with no strikes against us.

I've thought hearing the phrase "failure is not final" was the starting point of my introspection, the first motivation to believe I could overcome all which has constrained me. But, well into the writing of this book, I remembered writing my answer to this intriguing question I found on the internet a few years ago. "Suppose you could go back in time to talk to yourself at the age of ten. What advice would you give to yourself?"

Remembering this revealed what I've come to understand in my transition from darkness into the light. At the time, I had no confidence in the Spirit's working of all things for good. I was living in emotional darkness and spiritual malaise. I was trying to force a course for my life which would not and should not be. Certainly, it was not my course according to God's plan. I could not yet see or trust His working in my life. But, God had begun His work. He saw the time was right. He saw I was almost ready to try a different way – His way. In writing to myself as a ten year old boy, God was beginning to teach me His "all things for good."

"Paul, at age 53, would like to tell Paul at age ten, 'The really great blessings of this life are not the BIG blessings. Oh, sure, when you say your prayers through the years you'll say, 'We thank You for our many blessings,' and you'll mean the big stuff. Aw, you know, your house, your car, your clothes, your job; all the stuff you just know you gotta' have. But, believe me, someday when you've gone through all the years which will either toughen you up, or maybe tear you down, it will hit you – the real blessings are in the little things. The little things which you may not even notice now; those things which people do for you or give to you which seem small, but will actually shape who you are forty years from now.

There's stuff that's already happened to you that when you are old will mean a lot to you. Stuff like, well don't you remember the time back when you were five, and for some reason Mom didn't have a car to take you'll to church one Sunday morning. Remember when she got you all dressed up and you'll walked to church. You haven't thought about it since, but someday you'll realize just how big a deal that was. You'll know the morning's walk taught you something very important. Yes, someday you will say, 'That Sunday, and what my

Mother taught me about the importance of going to church, is why church is still important to me.'

I know you really like to sing. At night while you are going to sleep, you'll sing. Ben will make fun of you because when you sing a church song, at the end you'll make sounds trying to imitate the sounds of the last few notes the pianist plays. He always thinks it's so stupid, but don't mind him. Anyway, when you are old you'll still be singing, probably leading the singing at church. By then you will understand the importance of small blessings, and you'll know why singing is still important to you.

Don't you remember back when you were about that same age, or maybe six, and the preacher's wife would let you sit on the bench next to her while she played? You really loved that, didn't you? Well, someday, believe me; you'll know the experience is partly why singing is so important to you. Yep, you're gonna' know then it really is the little blessings which we should be thankful for.

So, try to notice more of the little things. Things like how much your Mom and Dad are giving of themselves to try to make your childhood special. Believe me, someday when you have raised your kids (Yes, you will have some!) you'll wonder, 'How did they do so much?' Your folks will make some mistakes, but they will try so hard.

Oh yeah, there's something else. I know it's hard for you growing up with your older brother, but try to understand him. I mean it; really try. I know he hurts you and it's hard to hear people talk about him, and darn it, I know he wrecks so many family times. But, try real hard not to hate him. Really, the hate is not good for you. The hate will just make so many things harder to understand someday. But, that's enough of that.

Guess what; someday you're going to have a really great wife! Yeah, really! And, she'll be one of the big things you're thankful for when you say those prayers. She'll be the one to help you understand it's the small, seemingly insignificant things which are the greatest blessings. (Say, kid, do you know what insignificant means? That's just the little stuff.) It's the little stuff she'll do for you that will make your life good. In the early years you'll know how much you love her, but you won't know just how much until maybe thirty years, or so. You'll really need her. She'll carry you through so much. You lucky dog, she'll believe in you way more than you believe in yourself. She'll make you better than you are alone. Listen, Paul, you'd better try to do the same for her because just like your parents are having trouble with your brother, you may have your own troubles with your kids, too.

So, come on, Paul, try to see all the special little blessings, and remember them. Someday you will know just how much they will have shaped your life. You'll get all hung up on trying to accomplish the BIG things, but really, believe me, it's the little things you'll cherish when you get old.

Oh, yeah, before I forget – take more care on that math homework, you'll need it. If you don't, someday you'll really be peeved with yourself.

Hey, kid, it really is gonna' work out in the end. Really! So, don't worry about it so much! It'll be okay, Paul.

How about we get together and talk it over in about forty years or so? Then you can tell me more of the little stuff I should have noticed along the way. See ya' soon! Yeah, it'll be sooner than you think."

Indeed, it is the little things through which God can work His good will as we press on toward higher ground, toward the higher calling of God, and past spiritual mediocrity. By His hand, we'll gain new heights every day; until the day when we reach a plane higher than we have ever found, because Jesus has just planted our feet on Heaven's ground!

> *Lord, lift me up and let me stand,*
> *By faith on Heavens table land,*
> *A higher plane than I have found;*
> *Lord, plant my feet on higher ground.*

TWO

UNTO A NEW SONG

Our journey as Christians would benefit from a little more day-dreaming. Amid the striving to know more of God through His Word, and striving to live more as He wills, we may be missing the blessings of simply daydreaming. Yes, just daydreaming about His promises to us. We often sing of Heaven, of how wonderful it will be; the eternal home of the soul! Yet, how often do we let our thoughts dwell upon Heaven? How often do revel in awe of the glories of Heaven?

We sometimes sing a wonderful song in our worship. Many days, when I think about Heaven, these words richly ring in my mind:

> *On Zion's glorious summit stood*
> *A numerous host redeemed by blood!*
> *They hymned their king in strains divine;*
> *I heard the song and strove to join,*
> *I heard the song and strove to join.*

The simple phrase, "and strove to join," paints a beautiful picture of our yearning for the first glimpse of Heaven; the description found in the opening verses of Revelations 14. John saw, as we hope to see, "There before me was the Lamb standing on Mt. Zion. And I heard a sound from Heaven like the noise..." Let yourself envision the picture these words paint, "the noise of flooding water, and like the sound of loud thunder. The sound I heard was like people playing harps. And they sang a new song!" Yes, a new song like none ever rose before. I like to daydream about it, imagining the day when, perhaps, even from a distance we will hear that mighty chorus! We'll hear the song like mighty, rolling thunder, and strive to join.

If you've lived in parts of the country where it thunders violently, you remember the concussion literally shakes the foundation of your home. I imagine the sound of the New Song will be like the roar of the mighty thunder; a sound which will cause the foundations of the universe to rumble and quake.

Let yourself imagine it; imagine the indescribable joy! Can you see it; really, can you see it? It's hard to see it in this life, for even in our moments of highest joy, we cannot imagine the joy of that day. Here our joys are tempered by the burdens of life, tempered by bearing one another's burdens, and tempered by the struggle submit our burdens to the Lord.

But, in that day our joys will know no bounds! As I look forward to the joyous day, I recall a phrase from, *How Great Thou Art;* "then sings my soul." Those four words paint a beautiful emotion. "Then sings my soul" is about a song which comes not just from the lips, but from the depths of the soul. It is a song not just of the mind, but from the bursting of the soul in unbridled joy! When bearing the burdens of this life are past, yes, then sings my soul. When this body suffers no more, yes, then sings my soul! When the final battle of sin has been won, oh yes, then sings my soul! It is in that joy when I will first hear the mighty chorus sweetly singing. I will hear the song and strive to join!

Certainly, in this life there is no equal to that day. It is, perhaps, vulgar to compare anything to the wondrous joy of that glorious day. Imagining such joy may, in a small way, be akin to the anticipation we feel before a huge sporting event. We can imagine this – the football season's final game; perhaps, the ultimate rivalry of two unbeaten powerhouse teams. This day, one will be the victor in the spotlight of sport's glory!

Now imagine it – you've spent a small fortune on these tickets. In the crush of traffic to get to the game, you're running late. The game has already started. The play-by-play is blacked out on the radio. You're missing the game and dying to know what's happening. Finally, you arrive and from far across the parking lot you can already hear the roar of the crowd. Entering the stadium, you hear and now you can even feel the thunder of the crowd. You hear the sound and strive to join! And, when you see the field, in the excitement of the game, you'll see your team is winning. Your voice will rise and join in the roar!

That's a shallow substitute for the pure joy we'll know when we hear the mighty chorus sweetly singing a new song; a song which will be forever new, a song of praise to the Lamb. A never-ending song in adoration of the Father, a never-ending song in thanksgiving for the Son, a never-ending song of Eternal Joy – a mighty chorus which forevermore will swell and ring!

While First Corinthians 2:9 is not about Heaven we relate the words with Heaven. "No eye has seen, no ear has heard, and no mind can imagine what God has prepared for those who love Him." Certainly, we can't imagine it. And, God doesn't tell us much about our heavenly home. We are promised eternal rest, eternal joy, and eternal rejoicing. "He will wipe away every tear from (our) eyes, and there will be no more death, sadness, crying, or pain, because all of the old ways are gone" (Revelation 21:4). We are assured Heaven will be like a hidden treasure, to be prized as one who finds a prized pearl of great value.

The Word reveals glimpses of Heaven in Revelation 4 and 5. We read of the throne of God and see the Lamb that was slain, now standing on Mt. Zion. We know that in this new city, we, the church, are the perfected bride of the perfect Son of Man. Amen! We will not find any temple built there, "because The Lord God Almighty and the Lamb are its temple." There is no night because, "The city does not need the sun or the moon to shine on it, for the glory of God gives it light, and the Lamb is its lamp." Unlike this world, "Nothing impure will ever enter it, nor will anyone who does what is shameful or deceitful, but only those whose names are written in the Lamb's book of life."

What we desire most is there, for we will find the throne of God and the Lamb in that city. We "will see His face, and His name will be on (our) foreheads." And in the land of never-ending day, we "will reign forever and ever." Then we will see the fruition of our faith, in that city called, "The Lord Is There" (Ezekiel 48:35).

Its glory will be beyond anything I can imagine, but this makes me want to know more. I think, "Tell me more, God." But, should I really let myself dwell so much on Heaven? How much should I look towards Heaven?

As Christians, we sing "There is much to do; there is work on every hand." We are called to do much as Christians. First, we are called to glorify God in all things. Within this call we are told to "seek and save," and to "watch and pray," and to serve Jesus and others before and beyond ourselves every day. So, should we be dreaming about Heaven? Absolutely, yes!

The gospel of John tells us why, for there we see the promises of God and the fulfillment of all prophecies are in the crucible. John's gospel places us at the crossroads of all scripture, seeing the passing of the old order of Law and the coming of the new order of Grace.

The gospel of John is where we come to trust in Jesus through the many wonders proclaimed, and in the accounting of prophecies fulfilled. But, I hold the book to be much more tender and personal. Perhaps, as tender as the Song of Solomon, from which we remember the story of Solomon and his maiden, in the flowering of their love, their courtship, and their marital intimacies. Some people believe their relationship is an allegory of Christ's love for His bride to come, the church. If the Song of Solomon represents Christ and his bride, I believe the gospel of John is the stating of the marriage vows – Christ's sacrifice leading to the birth of the church; the church prepared to be the spotless bride of Christ. John's gospel is an account of spiritual intimacy between Jesus and the twelve men ordained to nurture his bride.

The final discourse of Christ in the hours prior to His crucifixion is the intimate instilling of all which the apostles must hold in their hearts to sustain them in their mission. We must remember, these twelve ordinary men had no long spiritual heritage with Jesus – they were common men of common skills and trades, newly called to Christ's purpose. Prior to the day of His death, at the crux of the Divine Plan, Jesus had to intimately indwell their minds with All Truth. It was to be the apostles' mission to bear and sustain His mission.

I view Jesus' discourse intimately because it seems very much like the deeply cherished time I spent with my mother in the hours before she died. She, like Jesus, knew the time of her death was at hand. She knew that she would soon be leaving those dearest to her. We spent our time together sharing last messages each of us needed to know. We shared intimately from our hearts of the truths of our lives, and of the truths she wanted me to cling to for comfort. Her purpose was to set my course ahead based on all she had taught me, and all she knew I could become. It was a deeply treasured, life enriching, and intimate time. And, like the apostles with Jesus, my final hours with Mom held much of our truth which sustains me now.

During those final hours Jesus instilled in His Apostles His Father's will for their course. All Truth hinged upon setting a sustaining light within the hearts of the Twelve. They would have to own their roles which had been ordained by the infinite "I AM," and understand the prophecies were being proven.

By our experiences, we hold some days as days of infamy. December 7th, or 9/11; we don't even have to say the year. Oh, how slight those days are when held in light of the day which truly changed the course of this world. As the Sacrifice made perfect through obedience to God's plan, Jesus must make the apostles understand how their lives would change. These men were the intimate family of Jesus; could they really know how much their lives would change by forfeiting their livelihoods to follow Christ? Jesus had to make them understand, "The time of My departure has come" (II Timothy 4:6).

Quite intriguing are Jesus' oft repeated words, "I tell you the truth." Jesus who the Apostles believed, and who is the very embodiment of Truth, validated His words with, "I tell you the truth." To weight the keys of the gospel which the Apostles must carry in their hearts, Christ emphasized, "I tell you the truth."

Only once did Jesus vary the preface, seemingly as a means to be doubly emphatic. Speaking of all which He will prepare in Heaven for those who love Him, Jesus says, "If it were not so, I would have told you" (John 14:2). Among His last words to share, Jesus wanted the Apostles to be convinced, "In my Father's house are many rooms." Because Jesus knew full well how the Apostles' lives would change after the crucifixion, He wanted them to know the assurance of an eternal reward. Jesus knew that some days His purposes exercised through them would be sustained by His words and, perhaps, a little daydreaming about the promised glories of Heaven. Yes, I believe we are to set our sights upon Heaven.

If Heaven merited Jesus' double emphasis within the final discourse with the Apostles, why doesn't the Bible tell us more? Wouldn't a greater revelation of Heaven instill a greater desire to obtain Heaven? We are told no more about Heaven because God knows our human nature. It is within the basic nature of man to seek the highest and best for ones' self. Simply put, we hold well to the notion of keeping our eyes on the prize. We are prize driven, rather than purpose driven!

By human nature we don't want to persevere through the trials. As we sing, "If for the prize we have striven, after our labors are o'er; rest to our souls will be given, on the eternal shore." The chorus is about seeking Heaven, yet includes, "Oft in the storm, lonely are we, sighing for home, longing for Thee." We'd rather dodge the storms of life; thinking, "Jesus, just give us our prize."

Publishers' Clearing House proves our prize-driven nature. How many people have subscribed to a magazine because of a slimmer-than-slim chance of winning ten million dollars? We are told, "No purchase is necessary to win!" But, we think the odds have to be better by subscribing. We buy for the remotest chance of winning. However, by basic human nature, how many people find it hard to subscribe to an assured home in Heaven, guaranteed by the immutable promises of God?

Yes, within our earthly nature we are prize driven. In Matthew 13, we read Jesus' parable of the hidden treasure. "The kingdom of Heaven is like a treasure hidden in a field. When a man found it, he hid it again, and then in his joy went and sold all that he had and bought the field."

Following, we read another parable about the pearl merchant. "The kingdom of Heaven is like a merchant looking for fine pearls. When he found one of great value, he went away and sold everything he had and bought it." Would either of them have sold all they had without already knowing the prize? Would the man who found the hidden treasure have sold all that he had, buying the land just to toil in it, without the treasure? Likely not; his joy in the assurance of the prize made the land worth all he had.

It seems Christians seek too much of Heaven's reward while in this world. We are keen on the notion of receiving from God a wealth of blessings until our cup is full, "pressed down, shaken together, and running over" (Luke 6:38, which in context has nothing to do with money). We want more of His blessings now; for He did promise a life lived abundantly. But, God never promised us a rose garden. He never promised preferential treatment in this world. Rather, we are warned if we truly cling to Him, we will be hated and persecuted by the world. The "cup running over" does not promise riches in this life. He calls us to live contentedly in spiritual abundance by living within God's will, and unto the absolute abundance of a heavenly home.

As a poem, *Heaven on Earth*, I say it like this:

> *Oft, of the prize we yearn to know,*
> *Awaiting in Heaven, that fair land to go.*
> *No eye, no ear, no thought can ascend,*
> *To wonders wrought by the Son of Man.*

> *Thinking bright glory, here we should see,*
> *Health, wealth, and wisdom, our Heaven to be;*
> *In striving to do, we make Him small,*
> *If Heaven on earth holds all in all.*

> *Blessings in all things, God ordains,*
> *Unto each heart, where He lives and reigns;*
> *Yet, this no promise of thorn-less roses,*
> *Life by His power, His Word proposes.*

Some things we deem near heavenly,
Yet Heaven here can never be;
Here, no royal robe and crown,
Here, no angelic anthems sound.

The wait, the journey, and the race,
Sweeter still our meeting make;
When we know Him face to face,
We'll know full well His saving Grace.

Far beyond, far greater than we create,
True Heaven is well, well worth the wait.
Then in judgment, the appointed date,
New song singing, we pass thru the gate.

According to God's wisdom, we are to be purpose driven; that is to be "called according to His purpose." Then, by what godly purpose are we to dream of Heaven?

Because, we are assured by the words of Jesus, "I am the way, the truth, and the life; no one comes to the Father but by Me" (John 14:6). No one can enter a heavenly reward except through Jesus. Thus, the only way to dream of Heaven is to set our purpose upon Jesus' purpose. For "many are the purposes of man's heart, but it is the Lord's purpose that prevails" (Proverbs 19:21). It is easier to know the purpose of a man's heart, but it is only fine "to be zealous, provided the purpose is good" (Galatians 4:18); that is, a purpose which is of God. Jesus, who prepares our heavenly home, also provides The Way, and the mindset for seeking Heaven.

Philippians 3 tells us how to set our hearts on Heaven; to be purpose driven rather than prize driven. Paul, in his desire to share in the resurrection to eternal life, writes, "I want to know Christ and the power of His resurrection …" (v. 10). Yes, Paul is looking for that city, but he knows there is a purposeful process towards attaining what has been promised to him. He seeks the "fellowship of sharing in [Christ's] sufferings, becoming like Him in His death." Paul, acknowledging his imperfection, his purpose is to strive to become more and more like Christ. Paul's pressing on in his sufferings was to establish Christ's church, His Word, and His mission until that day of "taking hold of that for which Christ Jesus took hold of me" (v. 12).

As for me, Jesus knew my heart and my mindset towards worry and darkness. Jesus' words in Luke 12 speak against worrying, and speak to a purpose-driven pursuit of Heaven. He tells the people "Do not worry about your life, what you will eat; or about your body, what you will wear. Life is more than food, and the body more than clothes... Who by worrying can add a single hour to his life? If then you cannot do even this very little thing, why do you worry about other matters" (v. 25-26)?

Yes, certainly, life is so much more than just food and clothing, but whatever my worries are, the message of Jesus is the same. If speaking directly to me, Jesus might say, "Paul, why are you wasting so many years worrying about things you cannot change? Why are you burdened with the strivings for a better work, and a better life in this world? Besides, I have already purposed for you a better work, that work which brings glory unto my Father. And, why do you needlessly suffer in darkness under the worries for others and their strivings; have I not already proven my sufficiency in working all things together for good, both in your life and theirs? I tell you the truth, I will continue to do so, completing my good work in you, if you will but press on in the cause to which you have been purposed."

Pertaining to my goal of Heaven, Jesus might continue, "Paul, seek first His kingdom, and the desires of your heart will be yours. Yes, there is the prize to come, but to obtain Heaven you must trust Me for all things." Indeed, Jesus assures us His Father is pleased to give us the prize as each one trusts Him, and perseveres in the *purpose* of His calling, rather than the *prize* of His calling.

Jesus, taught His disciples by the parable of the rich fool. This man purposed to store up the wealth of his own success and achievements, and to depend on them to fulfill his needs for years to come.

Though not wealthy, I am too much like that fool. Perhaps, Jesus meant the parable for a dark worrier like me; anxious for accomplishments, for financial security, and fretful over elusive dreams not yet to be. His assurance is by trusting God for all things, and seeking first His kingdom, I need not worry. Ignoring the lesson of His parable, if I choose, I will only receive what I have prepared for myself – which is not a glorious prospect.

Similar direction is found in Colossians 3. Again, if Jesus was speaking directly to me, His words might be, "Paul, since you have been raised with Christ, set your heart on things above, where Christ is seated on the right hand of God. Set your mind on things above, not on earthly things." I had to learn and accept the things in my life which are not mine to change. Frustrated with my career, missed opportunities, and deflated dreams, I had to know my past goals were not meant to be. Now, by starting each day with, "I'm pressing on the upward way," and meaning the "way" to be Jesus' way rather than mine, the defeated depression has lifted, and continues to lift.

Colossians 3 continues to teach us, "When Christ, *who is our life*, appears, then you also will appear with Him in glory" (v. 4). There is the purpose which leads to the prize of Heaven – "Christ, who is *our* life." Living with Christ as our purpose means striving to be more like Him by putting to death "whatever belongs to your earthly body" (v. 5). It was my earthly nature which held me back in my Christian walk; held me to marking time rather than marching onward.

Colossians 3, as well as Luke 12, was the call for me to reject materialism, and to reject a focus on setting my riches in this world. Like the rich fool, my desire for the possessions of this world kept me from desiring a spiritually higher plane.

As a would-be architect, I'd always been fascinated by the descriptions of Heaven – the precise dimensions of the jeweled foundations, the radiant lighting, and the materials specified for every element. So intriguing in First Kings 6, are the minutely detailed instructions of God for the building of the temple. There was a definite purpose in building the temple according to God's design. The people earned the fulfillment of God's promises by following

His plan. Reading First Kings is like reading the Master Architect's specification sheets. Beyond building the temple according to His specs, it was about similarly building their lives in order to bring acceptable honor to God.

Perhaps, I was too fascinated in those details. For too many years I sought to design my little portion of the world, all perfectly proportioned, as if my plans would yield contentment. I obsessed in trying to make this life perfect, even though I knew it can't be. I spent years looking for a better town, for a better job, for better things; quite determined to make life perfect through those strivings. I spent countless days designing my notion of perfection, but really just to escape from my discontent.

As thoroughly as God specified the building of the temple, I poured myself into designing the perfect house, with perfectly proportioned rooms, and all the elements exactingly calculated to scale. It was a vain fascination, thinking I could create real contentment by my own hands. Such is the vain and abject foolishness of man!

Wisely, and gently, through the years my wife encouraged me to look for both a higher and a deeper means to find real peace. Confronting my desire to find greener pastures, she'd remind me in words I hated to hear, "Happiness is not a place on the map."

The cares and burdens of this life will always be an obvious presence. Burdens persistently have a way of pushing the higher passions, purposes, and promises out of our lives. But, as burdens press, we can look upon the Great Day Coming as a means to bear the burdens. Setting our hopes on things above, and a little dreaming about Heaven, really can help. The challenge is to hold to all which God has purposed for us in this life, trusting Him for the glorious prize in the life to come.

We should set our minds on Heaven because God promises Heaven to those who diligently seek Him, as an eternal reward of our spirit. Remember, the promise of Heaven is at the core of Jesus' final discourse. Remember Jesus' words, "If it were not so, I would have told you" (John 14:2).

We are Christians, having put on Christ for the remission of our sins. We are saved, but, saved unto what? Beyond the call to glorify

God, why do we seek forgiveness? Are we saved from death unto life only in this present life, then to simply lie eternally in the cold, dark ground? Indeed, not!

We are saved towards obtaining the ultimate goal of Heaven! We are saved to reign with Him through endless ages, in praise, in peace, in pure joy amid the powerful chorus of the redeemed. We are lifted up to sing a new song, in glory forever, and ever more! Oh, yes; "then sings my soul!"

THREE

A FEW SKIPPED BEATS

All of Creation and all of life is rhythmic; patterns of days and waves. We depend upon rhythms; the cycles of seasons and currents, of life and death. We are balanced, we are ordered, and we are secured by rhythms.

Life, like music, breaks when rhythms break. As a small child, I knew the predictable rhythms of life would skip a few beats along the way. Now, the memories of the missed beats only have value by their affirmation of God's working in my life, and of Jesus righting the broken cadences, helping me get back into step.

The rhythms which brought me to this introspection are, in some ways, as dark as Heaven is light. It would be much easier to simply testify Jesus is sufficient to meet all my needs through His benevolent mercies and matchless grace. But, a credible affirmation of His power requires some revelation of the darkness through which His Light penetrates.

Perhaps, in the whole scope of human tribulations, my darkness was merely a cloudy day, in comparison to another's utter darkness. In the average of childhood journeys, mine was largely just that – average. But, average isn't easy for a kid with a fear-based personality. Yet, in the mean, and in the deep shadows of far worse, I can now see God was always near; at least as near as I would draw to Him. It is the deep shadows though which led me to search for light, both in Jesus and in looking for that city.

My purpose is not to celebrate the darkness, for there is far too much of that already. It is the mindset of our society to revel in the lowest common denominator of mans' character and travails. It seems to be a common trait of mans' nature. At one time it was my nature, to fixate only on the negative and negate the positive.

Who can see a single speck of darkness in the brightness of the noonday sun? However, within the utter darkness of a deep cavern, one can see a candle's flickering far into the abyss. Therefore, in my purpose of celebrating light instead of darkness, I've struggled with the question of how much darkness to reveal. I've resolved to grind no axes, to cast no sadness on the living, or to heap no shame upon the dead. Casting darkness on others is in no way a celebration of Jesus' light.

If I'd spent as much time understanding what God purposed for my life as I have in just trying to understand me, God could be so much closer in completing the good work He began in me, toward perfecting it unto the day of Christ Jesus (Philippians 1:6). Still, I wonder why some can see a glass half-full while others see it half-empty. Far broader and deeper minds than mine have yet to fully answer those questions. But, for those like me, who by a melancholy nature anxiously view the world so darkly, we yearn to know why and how to change our outlook.

I believe one's outlook and personality are largely shaped by the vast gulf between what we believe life should be, and what we know this life is. The half-full or half-empty mindset is shaped by one's perception of the gulf, and how to bridge the gulf. Do we resign ourselves to remain on the life-as-it-is shore, or exercise the will to reach the life-as-it-should-be shore? Finding the answer may spur one to step out; to move from marking time to marching onward.

My outlook was shaped by the desire of making as few waves as possible in the gulf. There were desperate lives in the waves around me. While I added my moments of childhood mischief, there was a self-willed rein on getting into trouble; anything to keep from making waves. I knew my folks had enough to handle without adding any burden to theirs. Oh, I added some, but I never let myself forget it either; purposing even more to just keep the peace. Through the emotional illnesses of others in my family, through the complex tragedies of an older brother's life, and other trials yet to come, I wanted peace at all costs.

Early in life I judged the billows were too high; not at all certain I could rise above them. I feared being overtaken when the waves broke. This assessment planted my feet deeply into the sand of the as-we-know-life-is shore. As a kid who could obsessively dream of so much more, this concession early in life left a wide remainder of life to live in discontent and depression. Sadly, it took forty years to learn Jesus has waited to lead me across the turbulent gulf.

There is a mighty gulf between who God wills each of us to be, and who we know we are. The difference is a roiling river of sin and temptation which Jesus, and only Jesus, can span. Personality and perceptions aside, Jesus is the perfect span, and the Perfect Sacrifice, to take us over the river of sin. He lived fully, and was tempted fully as a man, becoming the Perfect Sacrifice through obedience to His Father's plan. He knew no sin, but has clearly seen the mighty gulf which only His Father's love and grace can span through His sacrifice at Calvary. Following His Father's will, Jesus' blood built the bridge over the river; and His life shines its light along my way.

As I've sung through the decades in worship:

> *O, the love that drew salvations plan!*
> *O, the Grace that brought it down to man!*
> *O, the mighty gulf that God did span, at Calvary.*

I've known the plan for so long, and have loosely counted on it towards the appointed day of obtaining my heavenly home. Only recently though have I, in pressing on to higher ground, purposed to live according to another verse of that song.

> *Now, I've given to Jesus everything;*
> *Now, I've gladly own Him as my King;*
> *Now, my raptured soul can only sing of Calvary.*

The calling is not only unto salvation; it is to gladly submit to Him as my King. To Him, I am called to submit my will, my plans, my possessions, and even my outlook on this life. Having submitted, I could learn His plan for leading me from the life-as-it-is to the life-as-it-should-be shore. Therefore, in striving to rise above the billows, I fixed my eyes upon the Lighthouse who led me to both salvations' shore, and to the contentment of living within the will and purpose of God.

Within the mindset of gaining still-higher ground, I strive to see all God has done to sustain me amid the waves. In coming to know how the Spirit has worked all things for good, I can see more clearly across the gulf to the other shore; both in this life and towards that eternal shore to come.

For a boy who craved peace, order, and smooth waters, the divorce of my parents in a small town in 1965, amounted to a hurricane's tidal surge. The wished-for rhythm and order of life was swamped by the wave. My perceptions of the billows cresting high made a treacherous gulf before me, particularly as I saw lives barely afloat around me..

The waves rolled from how our family was judged by others, because divorce at the time was still big, shameful news. I learned what people thought by what their kids said in school. Then I saw the married fathers of the same kids hit on my Mom. I also saw people in the church pull away. Sadly, when some should have been the most supportive, building up my parents without scornfully judging them, they withdrew. As I've heard it said in regards to some churches, instead of helping, caring, and nurturing the hurting, sometimes they shoot the wounded. In all of it, I perceived a gulf I dare not cross.

My parents' challenges centered on the stresses of my oldest brother's ill and tragic life; dealing with their perceptions of the life-as-it-should-be shore, versus life-as-it-is shore. But, now looking back, even then God was there. Jesus knew each one's pain, and within the deep yearnings of each heart, in God's timing all things worked together for good.

I've described my Mother as "a testament of Strength and an exemplar of Grace." As to her strength – raising three boys alone, managing the extreme needs of the oldest while nurturing the needs of the others - she took on a heavy burden. Mom could put on a confident face. She was strong in many ways, but at times, amid the trials the confident face became a wincing mask.

I was very close to my mother, each of us comforting the other in our individual sadness. She really knew my heart and, though not as fully, I knew her heart. Sometimes I saw behind her mask. She concealed matters which should be hidden from a twelve year old, but I saw much of the burdens she hid behind her mask.

After long days at work, taking care of her sons, and doing all she could to maintain the rhythm of our lives, some nights I'd stay up late with her. Within our trusting bond, we talked. I don't recall the words we shared, but I do remember the shared tears. I also don't recall the first time I brushed her hair as we talked; not to fix it, but to comfort her. She seemed contented in those moments. Whatever words were spoken, they did not speak as clearly as the tears, or as loudly as the quiet.

While I tried to live without making waves, there were times when I was a hateful child. I was never hateful to hurt her, but I lashed out in shameful ways to others. I verbally lashed out at a neighbor who cared for us, or sadly to my grandmother who so often cared for us, doing her best to make life right, too. They were shocked by the words, but more shocked by me saying them. I was stirring up the waves. It was my anger about the skipped beats in life's rhythm which caused the stir.

It was in the evenings following those angry days when I sensed the grace of my mother. She did not lash out at me; she did not reciprocate in anger. Her words were few; words which rebuked, but did not scold harshly. Sometimes there were no words at all. She understood the hurt which created the anger. She carried the guilt for those days, creating in her even more the desire to resolve the pain.

Despite the divorce, God taught me many good lessons through the lives of my parents. Never did I doubt how much I was loved. While I didn't live with my Dad, I learned how much he loved us and wanted to make the rhythms right. He continually did far more than required by any decree, for he acted from sincere fatherly love, not by the court's commands. More than most boys learn from their Dads, mine taught me it was okay to love deeply, reveal your weaknesses, and when need be, even to cry.

We were all blessed by the remarriage of my parents nine months later. I saw two, still-faulty people striving towards a selfless love, and striving to honor their commitments to marriage and to their kids. From them I learned a powerful message about the worth of marriage. My parents were not perfect people, but to me they were made nearly so because they tried so hard to make their marriage right. They knew the importance of their marriage in righting the rhythm of our lives. This lesson has served me well as I met my wife, and in our thirty-five years of marriage since.

I ventured into my teen years with much of the typical, small town set of experiences – baseball, band, church, first job, first car and first girlfriends. Although much seemed so typical, the fiercest of secret storms whipped the waves around me. The tumult was by the making of my oldest brother's tragic perversions. The turmoil with him, and the shame of it, raised the cost of keeping peace. But, to do otherwise would have raised a tsunami.

Simple, youthful innocence was too soon swamped by wickedness. Without being warned of the dangers, some waters I innately knew were evil; evil but powerful and compelling. Powerful of itself, but more so when exercised through the manipulative forces of emotional, physical, and sexual abuse. And, still more powerful when the abuse was concealed by a veil called, "Making No Waves".

Too soon, too compelling and consuming was the war between what is evil, and yet so intriguing; that which is aberrant and abhorrent, awful and yet alluring. The sexual senses, when so early abused, both defiled and beguiled. The conflict perverted what is good, and subverted the constraints of evil. The subversion bred duplicity, confusion, and self-damning darkness.

Again, it is not my purpose to cast sorrow on the living or to heap shame upon the dead, including that deceased brother. I will not tell more of the troubled waters with him. Certainly not the specifics of the abuse, for the telling of it would overshadow the sum of everything else in this book. Instead, the gravity of it can be perceived through the wake of the storms.

From the conflict I learned the darkness of hate, not just an ill-tempered grudge, but an ill-willed and ill-intentioned hatred. Many years later, amid self-loathing emotions, I regretted not having ended his life while I was a minor, when by all likelihood I would have been found legally innocent. Someone could have, and someone should have stopped him from holding generations of our family emotionally hostage. Why did I not take the loaded shotgun he once aimed at me and finally stop him?

It took many more years before, in hindsight, I could see the advanced malignancy in my soul, still growing from the long-festering hatred. Legally innocent or not, if I had killed my brother, it would have become an insurmountable darkness.

I also learned by my brother how to be double-minded; that is, to wear a mask covering the truth of my life. I learned to exist in a separate world of my making within my mind. When life was turbulent, or when the memories alone were turbulent, I left to my own secret place, to an almost peaceful shore.

I'm not going to claim a total understanding of how the Spirit worked all things for good in the midst of the turmoil, or since. Surely, He did, for I am still here today, striving to better know Him and His will for me. God, I am now assured, will not let me suffer more than I can bear; always providing a means of escape. Just as God did for David, "He reached down and took hold of me … he drew me out of deep waters" (Psalm 18:16).

Am I saying God's means of helping me in that time was by escaping to another place of my imagination? This seems to be a thin reasoning of His working. Yet, for a boy who was given a creative nature by God, and who lacked another set of skills to deal with the darkness, I believe God used my escaping to shelter me in the storms. While in my heart, I was tempted to all manner of real vengeance against my brother, I can only understand God's presence in my struggle in light of First Corinthians 10:13. "No temptation has overtaken you but as such is common to man; and God is faithful, who will not allow you to be tempted beyond what you are able to bear, but with the temptation will provide the way of *escape* also, so that you will be able to endure it."

Contextually, the teaching in First Corinthians 10 is against idolatry. While vengeance is not considered to be idolatry, the persistent desire to avenge darkly occupied my mind as forcibly as any idolatry. I escaped the desire for vengeance by escaping to my other world. I would better have fixed my eyes on Jesus and Heaven, but escaping helped me endure at the time. Again, just as promised, God was working and meeting me right where I was.

There came many years when my glass was more than half full. In all the joys of marriage, precious children, and a wonderful church family, life was good; better than I could see. Yet, along with the dreams planted in the fertile soil of youth, much of the darkness was planted, too. Some dreams didn't bloom as planned, but the tougher weeds flourished.

Though outwardly living as a Christian, I was severely lacking in prayer, Bible study, and in seeking Jesus' leading. Entering my thirties, I was in dire emotional and spiritual straits. Using the double-mindedness I learned as a teen, I lived very much as the Apostle Paul described, except with far less gain. "The good I want to do, I do not do, but I practice the very evil I do not want" (Romans 7:19).

That is not double-speak, but is very much the conflict of a double-minded person. My life was a paradox, dark and conflicted. Depression held me in the trough of turmoil, between who I knew I was, and who I hoped to become. If I wasn't daydreaming of a different life, I was too often thinking of ending mine. Where I once sought mental escape, I began to think about physical escape - suicide.

My error in dealing with depression was in trying to create my own solutions; creating scenarios of how I wished for life to be. Those schemes could never be, and shouldn't be. But, in the disappointment of seemingly every escape, layer by layer, I ratcheted up the darkness. Depression became anger, anger became apathy, and apathy bred a deeper darkness, to a point where it seemed even the Word of God held no power for change. The vacuum of positive will allowed negativity to fill the void. The darkness continually deepened; blocking out any perception of light.

Seeking to fill the cold, dark vacuum of depression, the challenge was in trying to find the filling - if not Jesus, then what? Often I filled it with more anger, vicious sarcasm and cynicism, which shored up the darkness. There truly is no emotional vacuum; something always fills the void. Absent the gumption to fill the vacuum with the Word of God, Satan was and still is all too willing and able to fill the void.

For those in the church who, like me, have wrestled with emotional illnesses, most will recall hearing someone say, "Well, if you just had enough faith, you'd be just fine. You just don't believe." And, most will also recall bristling, at least inwardly, "Oh, shut the hell up! I have faith!"

It's one of the quick, slick pieces of advice Christians toss about, but it was an indictment I had to accept. It was true; my faith was weak, starving by a lack of feeding it by prayer and The Word. There are only those two ways to converse and grow with God. Lacking those, how could I confidently say, "Oh, I have faith"?

There I was, a young Christian husband and father of three, blessed well beyond most of the world, but living in rancid darkness. But, now looking back so many years, I can see the time as one when the Spirit's was working all things together for good, because I still loved the Lord, to the extent which I could understand His purpose at the time.

Still very much involved in at least the routine of the church, I was blessed when the elders presented a Focus on the Family film series entitled, *Turn Your Heart Toward Home*. I was in turmoil during the entire series, but through it God met my needs.

The last film included a song by which turned my thoughts around. The song, *Daddy, Please Find a Reason to Stay*, is about a father who was going to leave his family. In the tender insights of a child, the little boy tells his Dad, "If you need a reason to stay, let me be the reason."

Those words slapped me hard back to reality. I had these three, precious kids who I had to believe from my childhood experiences, would be much better off if I stayed. Suicidal thoughts subsided. This was the song God used to save my earthly life, so that now I am persevering in the call of saving, through Jesus' sacrifice, my eternal life. I am convinced today, twenty-six years later; the song is why, in the Spirit's working all things for good, I am still here.

The late 80's, led to a move of eighteen hundred miles for a new job and a new start. The coming years were a blessing in many ways – financial recovery from several very hard years, and the expectations of what may come. They were good years, all in all, but Satan was not finished yet. We soon met a different kind of turmoil – a disintegrating church family. This was due to a minister and elders who thought themselves wiser than The Word; turning their eyes away from Jesus to seek their own will. Tragically, this congregation turned away from truth, the Truth; their own words becoming exalted above God's Word.

Those who sought to persevere in the Lord's Way were cast as trouble-makers. When elders were begged to study again what the scriptures say, they refused. The congregation fractured with the deeply wounded spirits of many. Today, sadly, God is still dishonored there, for their worship is not according to Truth.

God was already well ahead of us, preparing for us a new beginning, and very rich blessings. Though many were wounded, we were never set adrift. Though the gulf was rough, Jesus was in our boat, leading us to the better shore. The Spirit was already working all things for good.

Nearby, there was a small remnant of another group who had known similar trials; yet still seeking to worship, both in the Spirit and in Truth. Finding them was akin to fresh water quenching the throats of spiritually parched souls. As we came together, we saw how many people from all across the valleys were thirsting. They were seeking a place to glorify God, and to bind together as the God-ordained church. People drove from an hour away in several directions, as if journeying to an oasis, for the one purpose of worshipping as we ought.

Looking back, I can confidently affirm again, The Spirit is pleased to work all things together for good for those who are called according to God's purposes. And, looking back, I found one of the reasons for stepping out and marching onward. God was proving His unfailing mercy in meeting my needs, even in the darkest hours, shining the Light of His Son along the road I now travel.

Having grown up in a church and depending on a loving church family, I find it hard to understand how so many believe they can spiritually thrive without the church family. Particularly, in the adjustments to a new place far away from our personal families, we depended on many to help us make our new home. Church was a means to worship God, but also a context to holding up and building up one another in the journey towards Heaven.

The dependence upon the care and encouragement of a loving family of God became crucial as we faced our son's crimes and imprisonment. His failings were of the nature of which the Apostle Paul warned in I Thessalonians 4:3-7. "It is God's will that you should ... avoid sexual immorality; that each of you should learn to control his own body in a way that is holy and honorable, not in passionate lust like the heathen, who does not know God ... For God did not call us to be impure, but to live a holy life."

There had been similar offenses, as a teen, when we carried the burden totally in secret from family, friends, and the church. We wanted no one to know, believing we had to bear it alone. However, this present offense was fully known to all, quite impossible to hide; which not until much later we would come to know was a blessing in itself.

All my wife and I wanted to do was run away, hide, and start our lives over in another place. Shocked and grieving, we could not begin to separate our son's offenses with what must have been our critical failures as parents. Running seemed the only answer. Starting over in another place, people would not know our failures. But, in those early hours of turmoil, we didn't realize the power of love in those who would not let us go. They knew running really meant being set adrift, and alone.

This recovery was arduous and long; complicated by learning much too late that our son, at the age of eight, had been sexually victimized by a teenager in our neighborhood. The first major step was in understanding our burden couldn't, and shouldn't, be borne alone or silently. We had to know we couldn't solve anything on our own. Admitting this, and turning all control over to God was the very beginning of His healing, and the means of the real escape His Word assures.

What then held me stagnant for decades? Looking back, there were plenty of reasons to have been reaching out to Jesus' leading. As I asked in the *Introduction,* what keeps a soldier of the cross from stepping out? Why did I take so long to confront the depression, and so long to accept His plan for me?

From my words about seeking a church to worship God in the Spirit and the Truth, I hope you'll know I tread very lightly with the notion of either adding anything to, or taking anything from God's Word. Very carefully, I will add a twist to Jesus' parable of the soils. In Matthew 13, Jesus explains,

"When anyone hears the Word of the kingdom and does not understand it, the evil one comes and snatches away what has been sown in his heart. This is the one on whom seed was sown beside the road." Jesus adds, "The one on whom seed was sown on the rocky places, this is the man who hears the Word and immediately receives it with joy; yet he has no firm root in himself, but is only temporary, and when affliction or persecution arises because of the Word, immediately he falls away. "And the one on whom the seed was sown among the thorns, this is the man who hears the Word, and it becomes unfruitful. "And the one on whom seed was sown on the good soil, this is the man who hears the Word and understands it; who indeed bears fruit and brings forth, some a hundredfold, some sixty, and some thirty."

There were periods when I was each type of soil. Perhaps, I was most like the rocky soil, but I will dare to add another soil type. Depression results in sour soil. Rich and fertile, but this soil is too heavy, too saturated with stale water which drowns the seed. Some seeds sprout, but the sour soil chokes the air from the roots.

It seems the hearts and minds of those struggling with mental imbalances of many types are like heavy, sour soil. The good seed planted in our minds which should help us flourish can only rot in the mire of our minds.

In the hours of trial, we are blessed and sustained by those who have both empathy and sympathy. People will strive to find the right words, but in depression, those words often fall into sour soil. In the darkness, far down in the trough of trial, words like, "all things work for good" can be hard to receive, and harder still to trust. The words are falling into soil which is soured and acidic.

I don't think I'm the only person who in those times hasn't fought the urge to hiss through clenched teeth, "Get out of my face; you don't understand!" The words of comfort, given as solace and encouragement, are dependent on the soil which receives them.

Obviously, Jesus' parable of the soil has little to do with raising flowers. He's teaching about making our hearts fertile to receive truth, and receptive to the nurturing of the Truth. How does soil become rocky, or weed choked? How does fertile soil become sour, too acidic for good to thrive? By the absence of the True Light, all of life is sour.

We can see people living in the turmoil of families which, generation after generation, continue to perpetuate their troubles. They seem to celebrate their troubles. Or, we know people who seem resigned to their emotional or spiritual weaknesses. We're perplexed by their mindset and may wonder, "Why don't they stop wallowing in their muck?"

The answers are in two parts; how one views that troubled gulf, and to what or whom they cling to in times of trial. In those times of darkness, when trouble seems to be pressing our backs to the wall; it is in our nature to either fight or flee. Neither option seems right, but in fleeing, to what or to whom do we flee?

First, many people just can't see across the gulf before them. They don't believe it's possible to move from life-as-it-is to the life-as-it-should-be shore. The Israelites so often turned back to their life-as-it-was existence just as they were about to reach their land of promise. They lost their will to see to the other side. They lost the assurance of God's promises to them. Therefore, they were willing to remain in Egyptian bondage, generation after generation, perpetuating their plight.

Secondly, is the matter of to what or whom we cling in the time of trial? The Israelites, who turned back in fear of pressing toward the Promised Land, filled the void in their faith by rationalizing their life as it was would be better than the life which God had promised. Oh, if they'd only let His promises fill the void. I for too long, in fear not unlike theirs, turned back to a recollection of old experiences, which prevented me from clinging to God's promises and the Spirit's comforting. If one does not have the focus to fill the vacuum with the Word of God, Satan is all too willing to fill the void.

Recalling my first solo as a teenager, *Fill My Cup, Lord,* spoke to God's filling of the void. Anxious about the distance to the better shore, we need Jesus to fill our cup of assurance.

> *Like the woman at the well, I was seeking,*
>   *for things which could not satisfy;*
>   *but then I heard my Savior speaking,*
> *"Draw from my well that never shall run dry."*

> *There are millions in this world who are craving,*
>   *the pleasures earthly things afford;*
>   *but, none can match the wondrous treasures,*
>   *that I find in Jesus Christ, my Lord.*

> *Fill my cup, Lord; I lift it up, Lord;*
>   *come and quench this thirsting of my soul.*
> *Bread of Heaven, feed me 'til I want no more;*
>   *fill my cup, fill it up and make me whole.*

In Revelations 21, we read about the life-as-it-will-be shore. When this life is past, there is no longer any gulf to cross. John writes, "I saw the Holy City, the new Jerusalem. And I heard a loud voice from the throne saying, 'now the dwelling of God Himself will be with them, and He will be their God. He will wipe every tear from their eyes. There will be no more death or mourning or crying or pain, for the old order of things is passed away."

Following, John added these words from the One seated on the throne; "To him who is thirsty I will give to drink without cost from the spring of the water of life." Therefore, until I cross the final gulf, my constant prayer will be, "Fill my cup, Lord; fill it up and make me whole."

FOUR

A NEW MIND

A new mind - for anyone who has battled the cold, dark vacuum of depression, it is an intriguing thought. Or, I often wished I could simply turn off my mind. In awful, chaotic days with my mind racing and emotions raging, I felt like the ball in a pinball machine. It seemed my thoughts were batted around by the flippers from every side, slammed into the pins of extreme emotions, ratcheting up the score, with anxieties ringing like the ding-ding-ding, until anger flashed hotter than the garish lights. TILT!!! All I wanted to do was unplug the awful machine!

Worse than the days of depression were the days of frenzied, social phobias, which felt like everyone was too close and too threatening. Yet, the phobias were never as life threatening as the depression – I could simply flee. Phobias never made me want to unplug. Yes, "unplug" sometimes meant suicide, but more often it meant, "Can't I turn off my mind?

Some people who seek to unplug the pinball game turn to drugs or alcohol. I never did because drugs demand giving up control. But, while mentally escaping to my secret, life-as-it-should-be places, I forfeited control as suicidal thoughts ingratiated themselves into my mind. By God's sustaining mercies, I never tried to completely silence my mind.

A new mind, one which perceives the world differently and is not racked in chaos, is intriguing. Barring a new mind, one may wish for a way to restart the old mind. Those old enough can remember when, in its heyday, electroconvulsive therapy, usually called "shock treatment," was valued as a means to start the mind all over again.

(No, that was not its use, but that was my gross misconception.) And, I recall thinking, "That might be the answer; just wipe the slate clean! Start all over!" I sought a mind which would have no color of its past, but is clear and calm, free of any recollection of past storms.

The idea of a newly, wiped-clean mind does not make it a new mind. Even if shock therapy yielded a whitewashed mind, it couldn't last. A whitewashed mind functioning within the context of old thinking patterns would quickly be soiled. The need is not for a new mind, but for accepting a renewing of the mind to conform one's thoughts closer to those of Christ. Just as Paul wrote to the church in Rome, "I urge you, brethren, by the mercies of God, do not be conformed to this world, but be transformed by the renewing of your mind, so that you may prove what the will of God is, that which is good and acceptable and perfect" (Romans 12: 1-2).

The renewing of the mind, from depressed to balanced, means renewing our thought patterns, changing our focus and looking more directly on the matters of an eternal nature. It requires seeking more the will of God rather than seeking success, or dwelling on the cares which "so easily beset us" (Hebrews 12:1). It requires focusing our thoughts on things above.

God is glorified more by an old mind which has been renewed, than by a new mind, or a whitewashed mind. The blessing of a renewed mind is partly in knowing the state of the previous mindset. As Jesus works through one's life towards the renewing of the mind, the previous state of mind is a benchmark, a means to measure how far His transformation has moved the mind. Just as the light appears brightest when compared to the darkness which it overcomes, there is a blessing to be counted when comparing one's old mind to a renewed mind.

What depressed people really need is a balanced mind. More than a new mind or a whitewashed mind, God's purposes in our lives are served best through a balanced mind. Ecclesiastes 7:18 teaches, "The man who fears God will avoid all extremes." Certainly, the evils which have been exercised in the name of God, or the heresies proclaimed as Truth, result from minds anchored to the extremes. When my thoughts veered to the extremes, I was most prone to depression and to sin. Therefore, as I pursued the Light, my aim was not for whitewashing, but for rebalancing.

Know it is in God's power to renew and balance our minds if we submit to His will, focusing on His purpose. Just as David wrote in Psalm 13, I've wondered, "How long must I wrestle with my thoughts and every day have sorrowed in my heart?" David answers the mournful question, saying, "But, I trust in Your unfailing love; my heart rejoices in Your salvation." Through unfailing love Jesus changes our thought patterns, renews our focus; far better than starting with a clean slate with no appreciation for His good working.

One obstacle to a renewed mind is the reconciling of conflicting values as a Christian seeking secular treatments. People, whose faith principles have taught them to trust Jesus for all things, are conflicted by seeking secular help. Depressed Christians perceive the veracity of their faith is suspect if they seek other treatment. Their depression then is weighted with more darkness, a supposed failure for not finding Jesus as all-sufficient; further oppressing their will to seek help.

I spent years feeling this guilt; a shame it seemed I deserved for my double-mindedness. The shame derived from perceptions about how depressed people are judged by others. It seems when someone has cancer, it is understood as a physical illness. If someone persists in willful sin, it is understood as a spiritual illness. However, if someone suffers emotional illness, it is judged to be a fundamental brokenness of character – a sort of mental leprosy which others fear to contract.

When one has cancer, loved ones gather closely to hug, nurture and pray. People want to talk about the prognosis, the treatments, and to share experiences. For those lost in sin, those committed to seek and save the lost are anxious to help. But, the emotionally ill are often held at arm's length. In spite of everything vulgar which is so casually discussed, we don't want to talk about emotional illnesses, even those of our loved ones. People, including those of the church, are reluctant to support the mentally ill. Most often, except for praying the church does not know how to minister to the needs of mental illnesses.

Admittedly, I may have misjudged how people view the depressed, but I also held other emotionally ill people at a very long arm's length.

While I'd willingly support a friend with a physical malady, I was not willing to borrow trouble from someone with an unbalanced mind. And, I should have known better!

A dear friend, after many years of mental trauma, was diagnosed as bi-polar. We had worshipped together for months, but I had decided early on to keep my distance. I treated her like a two-headed serpent, being fearful to look into one set of eyes, supposing the other head might sneak around to bite me. Frankly, that's a cruel view of a bi-polar person, and it is a view which makes the mentally ill of any description reticent to reach out for support.

There is a more balanced view about seeking treatment, while reconciling Christian values with secular interventions. The better way is to again remember, "The Spirit works all things together for good to those who love Him and are called according to His purpose." Yes, *all* things in His hands yield to His good will.

Several years ago, my brother Ben suffered a large, aggressive, and tenacious brain tumor. Following a successful surgery, his prognosis remained dire. In the months following, he leaned heavily upon, and was sustained by his faith in the Lord. He and all those around him prayed fervently. Ben fully understood the words, "all things for good." Besides surgery, there was chemo, radiation, and medications in myriad combinations. All things worked for good – he has lived well many years past all predictions!

Aren't the medications and treatments also tools of God? And, the doctors' skills did not negate his faith. Rather, than negating God's control, they confirmed God's working in *all* things.

However, in the darkness of emotional illness, when I was already struggling to reach a balanced mindset, the promise of "all things work together for good," only added to the imbalance. The words were like seeds drowning in soured soil. It took years before the promise could take root and flourish.

While I assumed many people perceived my illness as a fundamental flaw of character, in reality it was how I viewed myself. The conflict was largely a matter of pride; not wanting others to see the brokenness. So, foolishly the illness was carried alone, and deepened.

What I defined as a problem of conscience in seeking counseling was really a matter of not trusting my relationship with God. He wants my conscience to be healed for my well-being, so I may serve Him. "How much more then, will the blood of Christ, who through the Eternal Spirit offered Himself unblemished before God, cleanses our *consciences* from acts that lead to death so that we may *serve* a living God" (Hebrews 9:14). I had to trust, "The Lord is close to the broken hearted, and saves those who are crushed in spirit" (Psalm 43:5).

The challenge in reconciling faith with secular treatments was the result of thinking errors; more an issue of perceptions due to my unbalanced mind. As I learned years ago, there is a widely accepted set of thinking errors common among depressed people. Reconciling faith and treatment came by learning the thinking errors are not of the world's definitions, but have clear biblical parallels.

As we learn from First Corinthians 10:13, "There is no temptation which is not common to man." Or, as it is commonly said, "There's nothing new under the sun." As a Christian or as one without faith, this set of thinking errors is common to the depressed, and of those who suffer other extreme imbalances.

Among the professionals who have defined these thinking patterns, there is broad agreement, but some variation in the labels assigned to them. This set is an amalgamation of terms from several sources.

All or Nothing Thinking

The bedrock issue appears to be all-or-nothing thinking. It is the mindset which ignores, or chooses not to see, any shades of gray. A particular word or action is perceived as either all good or all bad. In this mindset which I often fought, an all-good day can become an all-bad day by one negative word or event. "All or nothing" is the burden of the perfectionist's mindset – if it's not "perfect," it is ruined. In relationships, when a person does something well, they're thought of as the greatest; on days when they fail, they're viewed as near worthless.

Jesus, and John writing of Jesus, could speak of matters as all-or-nothing, and in absolute terms; the absolute sovereignty of God, the absolute love of Jesus, the absolute Truth of the Word. The Bible can teach us about absolutes, as in the warning to be either hot or cold, for if anything between, we will be spewed from His mouth. Indeed, in many ways God is an all-or-nothing God. His creation from the beginning was for all or nothing – all good. He created man-kind in the mindset of all or nothing – all pure. But, since the fall of man, on our own we are at best lukewarm, without the redemption of Jesus. Since man was cast from the extreme perfection of the garden, we cannot deal in the extreme.

We must avoid thinking in the extreme. The extremes become the markers of our sinful nature, or of whom we belong. The extremes become the "all or nothing" of our kinship with Him. We can't live for God when our thoughts remain in the extremes, for then we are most prone to sin. All-or-nothing thinking gives us the rationale that if we sin, grace will more abundantly abound. What a vulgarity of the Divine Grace and of the sacrifice of Christ. But, within the purpose of Jesus, the differences between our thoughts and motivations, and the Absolutes of God are mitigated.

We can never be perfect as Christ is perfect, we can never love as Christ loves, and we can never forgive as fully as He forgives. Our brightest light in living for Him will only be a dim reflection of Him. Despite our faltering steps to live as we ought, through the grace of God in Jesus' sacrifice, the difference is resolved. Through Jesus, the faults in any thinking pattern can be resolved within the truth of God's Word.

Locked in all-or-nothing thoughts, I was seeking to control my life. The reins were held firmly in my grasp. The "nothing" part of the mindset said God is not big enough to love, forgive, and direct my life. I believe it is also the thinking of non-Christians, believing they are not good enough to "deserve" His grace. Thus, the person is still holding the reins, ignoring that only by God's grace is one deserving.

Facts vs. Feelings Reasoning

All-or-nothing thinking morphs into the thinking errors which set feelings in conflict with facts; reasoning based only upon emotions. The emotional reasoning convinces a person that life will always be this way, condemning the depressed to living on the life-as-it-is shore. This reasoning makes one only see the two percent which is negative, forgetting the ninety-eight percent which is positive.

It is a mindset which must be overcome as one presses on towards higher ground. Had the Apostle Paul submitted to this pattern of thought, he could not have written, "…forgetting what is behind, I press on to the prize for which I have been called heavenward in Christ Jesus."

Despite the evil done to him, it is the shining quality of Joseph that he did not depend upon emotional reasoning. He did not lose sight of God's purpose and promises. How different the outcome of the temptation by Potiphar's wife would have been. How different the measure of God's blessings on Joseph would have been if he'd settled his mind on the thought, "God has betrayed me at the hands of my brothers." But, Joseph did not submit to emotional reasoning.

Despite the sins of David with Bathsheba, he did not persist in a pattern of emotional reasoning, though for a season his emotions had reign of him. He wrote eloquently of the dark shame within his heart. "Evils beyond number have surrounded me; my iniquities have overtaken me, so that I am not able to see; they are more numerous than the hairs on my head, and my heart has failed me" (Psalm 40:12). But, he never condemned himself to remain in that dark mindset. Depending on the Spirit to renew him, he wrote eloquently of finding light.

"I waited patiently for the Lord; and He inclined to hear my cry. He brought me up out of the pit of destruction, out of the miry clay, and He set my feet upon the rock making my footsteps firm. He put a new song in my mouth, a song of praise to our God" (Psalm 40: 1-3).

Elijah lived darkly at times, submitting to an irrational pleading for death based upon his feelings of failure and exhaustion. Despite his heroic achievements in vanquishing the forces of Baal, Elijah's reasoning plummeted due to the stresses of battle, and the pursuit of the vengeful Jezebel. Alone in the wilderness, he sat down in the shade and gave in to an unbalanced mindset. In the depth of depression, Elijah prayed for God to take his life.

Unrealistic Comparisons

Another treacherous path of irrational thinking is making comparisons between others and yourself; an error which I often made. This error thwarted my persistence in my career, and in my service to the church. It was always possible to find someone who could do a better job, and the comparison often led to resignation.

The core error of this thinking is a matter of pride. The challenge to correct the error is remembering that God did not call me to serve better than anyone else. I am not to be the imitator of anyone else; only to be an imitator of Christ. He only calls me to offer my best, even if it is not the best among all.

Making unrealistic comparisons leads us to wonder how godless men prosper, seeing ourselves as not being not as richly blessed. While Christians are promised a life more abundant, we can falsely see ourselves as deprived while even the wicked thrive. The damning trap in this thinking is focusing on the things of this world rather than setting our affections on the things above.

Unrealistic comparisons falsely lead some in the church to believe they are not valued. They begin, as I did several years ago, separating themselves, submitting to the feeling, "Nobody really cares if I'm here." Soon, they fall away from the fellowship. It is a misstep which can be avoided by focusing on the talents God has given them, rather than on the perceived better talents of others. It is by believing that in the body of Christ, the church, the foot is as valuable as the hand; all parts of the body purposed to perform, supporting one another.

Filtering

Filtering is an unbalanced mindset which focuses on the negative aspects of a situation, allowing the predictions which lead to failure. My filtering was the opposite of optimistically seeing the world through rose-colored glasses; more akin to looking through shattered lenses. Filtering present opportunities through the memories of past failures fixes one's feet in place, preventing any stepping out towards a goal. Pursuing higher ground, my steps falter if I filter God's plan through my past failures. Instead, I should, "forget what is behind and press on to the goal." If I use a filter, it should be the assurance that "I can do all things through Christ who strengthens me" (Philippians 3:14).

Overgeneralization

An extension of filtering is overgeneralization. Dwelling upon a record of past wrongs and failures, one may think, "I always fail anyway; I'll surely mess this up, too." To adopt this thinking into our salvation experience would be to doubt that grace can ever make me more than I have been. It forgets Jesus came to redeem us from past failures. Overgeneralization ignores God's grace; likely causing us not to stand up again after we've fallen.

Overgeneralization constrained my service to the church. Works which I once attempted were intimidating to restart. Other works which I barely started were not fulfilled due to the fear of failure based upon the past. Conversely, overgeneralization has been a problem due to the fear of success; the expectation that success in some endeavor requires greater efforts to follow in ever-increasing expectations. But, isn't this inherent in the concept of pressing on to higher ground? From either perspective, I let overgeneralizations prevent me from marching onward.

I come to the heavy hitters in my thinking errors lineup – "catastrophyzing," personalizing, and labeling. These were the most spirit-breaking and self destructive of thinking patterns.

"Catastrophizing"

Catastrophizing is making a mountain out of a mole hill. This thinking error betrays the central premise for this book. "God works all things for good for those who love Him and are called according to His purpose." Inflating our own mole hills disregards the Spirit's power to work all things for good. Biblically, the grand champions of catastrophizing may be the Israelites as they journeyed towards the Promised Land.

By the direction of God, Moses led the people towards the Red Sea. Looking back, they saw Pharaoh's chariots racing towards them. Within God's leading through Moses, according to the promise of their deliverance, many of them were ready to remain in Egypt as slaves. From the sight of the chariots they believed their death was certain. The chariots were their mole hill; the expectation of death became their mountain.

Later, in the wilderness they were hungry. By the direct provision of God they received manna and quail. Yet, even the provision of God didn't satisfy them; they were ready to turn back to slavery. Due to their discontent, and willingness to return to Egypt, hunger was their mole hill; thoughts of starvation in the wilderness became their mountain.

Possible catastrophes burdened their minds, but let's not think we'd react much differently. The hindsight of two thousand years may cause us to think we'd steadfastly trust God's promise and provision. Maintaining a balanced mindset in regards to the Israelites, we must remember their history. All they had known for four hundred years was slavery. Being slaves was more than the state of their existence; it became their identity.

Akin to their situation, some prisoners after being confined for many years become institutionalized. The bars which confine them now also confine their minds. Like the Jews in Egypt, being a prisoner is more than their existence; it becomes their identity. Likewise, for those suffering emotional illnesses, we let it become our identity. We "catastrophize," making our illness define who we are, rather than a transient state of existence.

Personalizing

My next grand-slammer of thinking errors was personalizing. For anyone who takes seriously their career, their marriage, or their role as parents, personalizing can be a self-defeating mental trap. Particularly for my wife and for me, learning of our son's offenses which led him to many years of incarceration, self-blaming thoughts seemed inevitable. "Surely, we did something wrong; we could have done better." Or, "Oh, I know we should have seen this coming. I would have done more to confront him."

You see the pattern developing, "we could have," "I should have," and "I would have." The phrases are the thinly-veiled blaming of ourselves for his mistakes. The "couldas, wouldas, and shouldas" sap the joy out of life. They're all about doubt and regret and the past, trapping our minds in perceived failures, and setting up the expectation of more failures.

What's the self-condemning trap in persistently asking the questions; I could have _____, I would have _____, and, I should have _____? Dwelling on those answers is dwelling in the past tense of our lives. Those answers ignore Jesus' purpose to redeem us from our pasts, so we will live more abundantly in the present.

The promise of God's grace reaching me holds the assurance He has already resolved the "couldas, wouldas, and shouldas" of the past. The message of grace includes the past is past; by grace we can leave the past tense of our lives. Grace promises the slate is washed clean, and has no bearing on the present tense of our lives. By grace we can learn from our past, and then live in the present tense of His continuing grace. Depend upon Him for the present, and purpose to live for Him unto the future tense of our heavenly home.

In a wider circle than my experience, I've seen the error of personalization be the cause of a preacher giving up his ministry. Though putting his whole heart into the work, but seeing disappointing results, he may personalize the lack of success as being his entire fault. Or, personalization may lead a child to blame himself for not saving his parents' marriage.

Labeling

Perhaps, my most persistent and self-destructive thinking error was labeling. Coming to understand this was a troubling process. Several years ago, in a terse exchange with my younger, teenage son, he retorted, "Why do you have to call people names?" In hindsight, taking the emotion out of the situation, he forced the valid question, "Why do you label?"

As I tried to control aspects of my life which are not mine to control, I used labeling both defensively and offensively. By labeling, I could set the boundaries of interaction with others.

Plainly speaking, labeling is prejudice; always a risky thing, and in the extreme, it's a spiritually deadly thing. Prejudice, or labeling, is exactly the mindset of Nathaniel when he asks Steven, "Can anything good come out of Nazareth?" In Nathaniel's thinking, the Messiah surely could not come from Nazareth. To him, Nazareth is akin to our thinking someone is "from the wrong side of the tracks; nothing good comes from that part of town." He saw no reason to interact with a Nazarene. Had Philip not insisted, "Come and see," Nathaniel may have missed the Savior.

This tendency to label is not always a bad thing. Sometimes it is good and needful. To the extent we need to assess the intentions of others, it is beneficial. Studies are revealing that children as young as six months are able to judge the basic goodness or evil in people. They already read expressions well enough to label people in whom they can trust and feel safe, or not.

Each of us, even those with a well-balanced mindset, uses these assessing insights. In the briefest of moments when meeting someone new, we are instantly evaluating and judging each other, deciding just how much of ourselves to offer to the other person. We're deciding how much to trust them, or how firmly to hold up our guard. Will we share similar views, or do we need to prepare for a fight? All decisions are based on appearances – clothing, hair, and body language. And, all those decisions amount to labeling. In the proper measure it is needful; in the extreme it becomes hateful.

If I label others in negative terms, it wrongly gives me an excuse to further judge them harshly, assuming that I know their motives and values. By labeling, I rationalize not having to deal with them. For one who thought of himself as not being arrogant, admitting I put others down by labeling was a big pill to swallow.

Labeling keeps one from admitting others can change. The label, usually derived from a perceived weakness in another, means we won't accept them even if they change. It's harmful to both, but more dangerous to the labeler. Through labeling we may miss blessings we otherwise can never know. And, the greatest danger of labeling is it blocks forgiveness. If I label myself as better than another, I can rationalize myself as being above needing to forgive another. The absurdity of that mindset is blatant. Even Paul did not consider himself above the worst of sinners, and Jesus' very purpose was to bring forgiveness.

Labeling kept me from seeing and pursuing many possibilities in my life. The persistent self-labeling of "failure" or "depressed" were the heaviest chains which constrained me from pressing on to higher ground. Not until I shed the patterns of these thinking errors could I firmly gain and hold to the higher ground God has planned for me.

The Fruit of Errant Thinking

Any one or all of the thinking errors devastates our joy as Christians because it keeps us from believing and accepting God's grace. Amid thinking errors, we sentence ourselves to a grace-less existence. In all-or-nothing reasoning, we're either loved by God, or we are not. By exaggeration, one fault makes us beyond the realm of grace. And, by personalization, we try to do all things by our own power, not depending on His grace to redeem us from our failures. It is not until God renews our mind, resolving our thinking errors that we can begin to understand His grace, and begin to accept His peace, which maintains the balance of the mind.

Gaining an understanding of the effects of thinking errors helped me understand the real nature of my depression. Those patterns of thinking so conditioned me as to even change my illness. From the depression grew a set of social anxieties and phobias. Actually, I'd be hard pressed to tell you which came first, the phobias or the depression, but within the depression I nurtured the phobias, until they became the larger problem.

The cumulative consequence of a mind so entrenched in thinking errors was essentially living absent-mindedly. An obstacle to renewing the mind was first reconciling my minds; joining together the mind I was regularly escaping with a renewed mind. But, the escape tactics I started developing as a kid, as an adult were perfected. I was the Harry Houdini of emotional escapists. There was rarely an emotional trap from which I couldn't extricate myself.

Despite my depression, some things about my life didn't mesh with the symptoms of depression. I functioned to a degree which belied depression. In job evaluations I was often told I worked harder than anyone else in the company. Only one other person ever scored as highly in an evaluation. It wasn't obvious that I worked absent-mindedly. I had so practiced my escape routines until I functioned well as double-minded man. I could work in this world while mentally absent from this world.

Mentally escaping was a benefit as a child; as an adult it was an emotional death trap. What served me well as a child now hindered me. I truly could not renew my mind until I understood the need to both live and think in *this* world.

The escaping started innocently enough – when there was turmoil around me, I escaped. When I was hurt, I escaped. If I saw someone hurting another, I escaped. When I saw people facing emotional tidal waves, I escaped. Seeing suffering always made me want to hide. Seeing the consequences of the suffering made me want to hide all the more. Eventually I spent more and more time "away." I was no longer escaping from any particular event; I wanted to stay away all the time. It is why I for so long loved architectural design. In designing "perfect" buildings I could live in a "perfect" place. In hindsight, I see long periods of my life when I rarely lived in this world.

The social phobias were born from my escapism. Remembering the situations from which I would escape and still dreading them, I lived in fear of conflicts, always with the expectation of "the other shoe dropping." If someone called or knocked at the door, I wouldn't answer it. Just because they called or knocked I had no obligation to answer. I thought "Whew – that's one conflict avoided." If I was asked to perform an unexpected function, I wouldn't. "Whew – that's another conflict avoided." "What, you want me to share someone else's burden – no way! Whew – that's one more conflict avoided." Soon I wasn't only avoiding conflict, I was avoiding *life*!

Finally, the other shoe dropped, and a few more shoes dropped after that. The thuds were too loud to ignore, meaning it was a time I couldn't flee. I'd have to fight, and fight hard. When the conflict really hits home, even one who lives in fear of all waves and deep waters will learn to swim.

Remember, I asked, "Why would a soldier only march in place, struggling against stepping out in full stride?" I was marking time in my life because I had built a wall of social anxieties around me. I've started marching onward by beginning to tear down the wall. But, it was not me who struck the first blows to the wall. It was God! I truly believe it was His working which helped me learn to fight when the big shoes dropped. And, from that fight, I eventually fought to overcome the darkness.

Much of the weight of tragedies derived from the nature of my son's offenses, one of the big shoes dropping. I dare to believe even those of a healthy mind, possessed of a positive outlook and a full measure of the Holy Spirit, would have been devastated. Much time was spent trying to understand the what, why, and how of his sin. Much of that was spent in coming to understand the thinking errors which beset my son; those thinking errors which constitute the assault cycle.

The Sin Cycle

The "Assault Cycle" is a chilling label to associate with your child. As I came to understand the thinking errors which led to my son's offenses, it was troubling to learn how his thinking errors perpetuated the assault cycle. Those thinking errors are common to his offense, but also to the widest circle of all wrongs inflicted upon another, including any sin of man. The assault cycle is identical to the mindset of mankind in any willful sin against God. The formally defined Assault Cycle is, more accurately, the Sin Cycle. The same thoughts which assault the laws of man also assault the laws of God.

The decision to commit an assault or to sin derives from a cyclical pattern of thinking errors. There is always a point in which sin is first conceived through either actual or imagined temptation. Following temptation, there is a critical decision to make – either cast the thought aside, returning to a balanced, healthy mindset, or dwelling on it, nurturing the temptation. The wrong choice nurtures the temptation, leading through several thinking errors, and to justifying the desire to sin.

We have a whole host of rationalizations. "Oh, no one will know." "It's not such a big deal; besides, I deserve it." "It will make me happy." By perverting scripture, the excuse is, "If I sin, God's grace can ever more abound."

If one does not break the cycle at this point, they are likely past the point of no return. They will commit the sin. In the midst of the brief, self-willed pleasure of the sin, one can be convinced of the lies. "I'm happy, and I deserve to be happy." This is the destructive and beguiling illusion of sin.

But, the pleasures of sin only last for a very short season. If one shred of a heart for the will of God remains, guilt will overwhelm the pleasure, and burden the spirit. Burdened by a load of guilt and shame, one must seek release from the spiritual storm. For release there must be another critical decision made – return to God, or to continue the cycle of sin. The wrong choice perpetuates the cycle. Thinking errors will again lead to the feelings one has a right to be happy; surely, God does not want anyone to be so sad. At this point, temptation will avail the means to feel better. And, once again, temptation gives birth to sin.

Scriptures prove the sin cycle. James 1:15 reads, "Then when lust is conceived, it gives birth to sin, and when sin is accomplished, it brings forth death." Job 15: 35 teaches, "They conceive mischief and bring forth iniquity, and their mind prepares deception." Similarly,

Psalm 7:14 reads, "Behold, he travails with wickedness and brings forth falsehood."

Obviously, it is no leap to reapply the premise of the assault cycle into the biblical context, but I must not equate the two. For "even the foolishness of God, [of which there truly is none] is higher than the highest wisdom of man" (I Corinthians 1:25). Still, there is truly nothing new under the sun; there is no sin which is not common to man (I Corinthians 10:13). The sins of this present age which we strive to understand through the Assault Cycle parallel the sins of the Bible; even the sins of the mighty men of God.

King David was accounted as having a heart for God, but it was not always so. While it was in the purposes of God to use David to accomplish His good will, David transgressed the law. Yes, David, from whom the wise King Solomon was born, and from whose descendents Jesus was born, was guilty of sins we describe today in terms of the Assault Cycle.

David's sins are told in the book of II Samuel. We read that while David had sent his troops off to battle, he remained at home. One evening, on his rooftop from where he saw Bathsheba bathing, he was tempted. He decided to sleep with her. The pleasure of his sin with her was short lived because she conceived a child. David then sent for her husband, Uriah, to return home from battle so he could sleep with his wife and to deceive who the father of her child was. But, Uriah, a loyal fellow soldier, did not consider himself worthy to enjoy the pleasures of home while the other soldiers slept in tents in the fields of battle. So, he did not sleep with his wife.

The first deception foiled, David chose to devise another falsehood. Inviting Uriah to dine with him, David deliberately made Uriah drunk, believing then he would go home to sleep with his wife. Yet, again, Uriah did not.

The pressure to cover up his sin was building. David concocted a scheme which led to Uriah being killed in battle. In the gall of deception, David claimed Uriah's death was merely a cost of battle, of no great consequence. Finally, thinking his deception complete, David sent for Bathsheba and married her.

David's sins are proof of the misdirected use of power in the assault/sin cycle. David's compulsions to sin are the core Assault Cycle motivations – to manipulate by his position of power, followed by manipulation to preserve his power. Rather than exercising his strength as a leader, his misdirected power exercised his weakness to sin. The brief pleasure of sin led to deception and more sin. David's thinking errors were running rampant.

David left himself wide open to the temptations of sin. The beginning of the story, in II Samuel 11:2, reveals the starting point of his sin cycle. "Now when evening came David arose from his bed and walked around the roof of the king's house." Why was he just getting out of bed in the evening? What was he doing walking around on the roof? He was bored to death while his troops were out in battle. He was idle, sleeping the day away and then prowling around looking for relief from his boredom. Surely, the king felt he deserved some relief, and by the sight of Bathsheba, sin held full sway. He thought of nothing better to do, and besides, he was the king. He deserved his pleasures.

David, very early in the sin cycle did nothing to avert his will from sin. There is always the point in the cycle when one must choose either to break the cycle or to perpetuate it. Beyond the feelings which lead one to temptation and to rationalizing their feelings, the first opportunity to break the cycle is the most critical, and David failed at the critical point.

However, when he returned to God's purposes, God could still use him for great things. God renewed David's mind and restored his place in His purposes. From David's deep shame, he pressed on in the mighty calling of God.

Ironically, the deepest pain of my life largely became the motivation for me to march onward within the vision of setting my eyes on things above. The wake of my son's imprisonment finally convinced me I'd have to turn my pain darkness over to Jesus' healing. I finally admitted, particularly in matters of my inner darkness, I would not be able to make sense of it on my own. Still, I did not step out to Jesus until I saw the Spirit's working inside the prison walls, in my son's life. Even there, God was, and is, creating in him a renewed mind. It was by the healing of my son's mind that I began to believe my mind could be healed. From his healing I began to see how God can work in all things for good. When I first heard my son speak truth, it confirmed the Truth.

Many question why God lets tragedies such as my son's sins happen. Without venturing here to answer the question, I hold to this – God in no way caused my son's errors. His sin was the result of living outside of the will of God, just like David, me, or anyone else. My son was enslaved by another master who from time to time, cast him into failure. However, God, can use the consequences of that tragedy for good, in my son's life and in mine. And, if by my efforts you are convinced of His "all things for good," God can work His good in you, too.

Certainly, we are skeptical of those confined in prison speaking of spiritual matters. We distrust their spiritual awakenings, and with valid reasoning. Compared to the earthly hell within the prison walls, it's not hard to understand their desire for a claim in Christ's promises. However, it's not only that I heard him speak truth, scriptural Truth, but I heard him speaking from the fulcrum of a balanced mind. With a renewed mind, he could admit his sins, and speak of his redemption from those sins. His was not a new conversion, but a recommitment to his conversion many years before. His renewal was restarting the efforts past salvation into transformation, reconciliation, and sanctification.

In balanced reasoning, he understands the consequences of his sin, the evil destructiveness of it, truly being accountable for the danger to others' lives. In balance, he holds to the optimism that beyond the social recompense he will always pay, beyond just knowing the Truth, it will take Jesus and the Spirit working in his life to resolve all the issues.

The mindset of our society is that those who have sinned in the manner he has should be buried under the jail. Those consequences of his actions are beyond his or my solution. He'll have to endure those with the Lord's help, hopefully regaining some measure of trust. But, it will always be his thorn in the flesh. For my son, just as for the Apostle Paul, the thorn in the flesh can be a reminder to keep him drawing ever closer to God. The consequences can draw him to darkness and to sin again, or as a thorn in the flesh it will lead him to follow Jesus as the Master of everything in his life.

God, in His infinite wisdom for mankind, can use people formerly guilty of great sins to further His purposes. Many there are who have sinned, but later returned to the call of God. Many, having once served their own desires ahead of God's desires, in God's timing went on to accomplish great things. It can be so with my son's sins, and my sins, coming out of darkness into His light. Jesus overcomes the darkness, heals us, and leads us into the working of God's will.

The Sustaining Light

Seeking a sustaining light which will illuminate my way has been a process of fits and starts. Simply put, it's often been two steps forward and one step back, but that's far better than no steps at all. It seems very much like the faltering steps of a new Christian, hopeful but fraught with missteps. Whether mental illness or salvation, overcoming darkness or sin, success hinges on the renewing of the mind.

In evangelism, many speak the words salvation and conversion interchangeably, as if they are the same. Salvation from sin and conversion to a new life are different matters. One cannot be truly converted without salvation, but one can be saved and not attain a lasting conversion.

Leading someone to understand sin and to recognize their need of salvation, they must be convicted of their guilt. Being truly convicted requires breaking down their old will, and their pride in their past way of living. It requires being brought lower in submission to the will of God. We may bring them to seek redemption from their sinful path, and they may truly of good conscience and fervent faith seek redemption through Christ. But, if we leave it there, it likely will not result in a complete conversion to a sustained walk in the Lord's way.

We teach them from what they must be saved; we often fail to teach what they are saved unto. Ultimately, it is to Heaven, but a new Christian will never make the leap without knowing which steps to take from there. We may lead them to salvation and teach them a theology, without teaching them how to sustain the walk. They gain a new birth without gaining a renewed mind. Remember the scripture, "Be ye transformed (converted) by the renewing of your mind." The former mind too often corrupts the new birth.

Newly redeemed Christians are like fish out of water. We may pull them from foul waters, but may not teach them to swim in fresh water. In the transition, they're likely to flounder and die.

The conversion of a depressed person from darkness into sustained light is much the same. Seeking a renewed mind, we know from what we want to be redeemed; we must know to what we want to be converted. Like a new Christian fooled by thinking their life will now be a rose garden, those striving to find light will be fooled by thinking any light will banish all their darkness. We must have a realistic expectation of what a balanced mind yields. It is not emotionally moving from thunderstorms to ever-blue skies. It is moving from storms to clear and partly cloudy skies, and a few more days of bright, sunny skies. In balance, every one receives and still needs a little rain.

Yet, within the times of a little rain, one can slip into a cycle of thoughts which lead to depression. Those thoughts follow a cyclical pattern similar to the assault/sin cycle, and they become an assault on a renewed and balanced mindset.

Typically, in response to something negative, either real or perceived, one of my thinking errors has a moment to engage. The "something" can be as small as an unexplained anxious moment. Or, it may begin within a thinking error itself, derived from taking my emotional pulse and expecting it to be a negative day.

If I haven't already, it's time to flip the circuit breaker, "I'm pressing on the upward way; new heights I'm gaining every day." If I, by purposing to think on higher things, do not break the cycle there, the likelihood of a darkening mindset and the likelihood of sinning increase. As I grow darker, I grow more anxious, sarcastic, cynical, or judgmental, and beyond being sinful itself, I'm near-surely going to fail.

Then, just as in the Assault Cycle, it is again decision time. I'll either, repeat the cycle and sin again, deepening the darkness, or I'll break the cycle allowing myself with Jesus' help to build a brighter and rebalanced mindset.

In the fits and starts of moving from darkness into the Light, I've been disheartened when the darkness so oppressively returns. After a period of many months, feeling like I was sitting on top of the world, (an unbalanced mindset in itself) I endured two days when anger, anxiety, discontent and darkness draped over my spirit like a heavy, wet blanket.

I used all the tools, trying to set my thoughts on things above; the pure, holy and true. I used all my sin cycle breakers, "I'm pressing on the upward way…" Again and again I sang, "I'll not be moved, I'll not be moved from Mt. Zion." It didn't settle the mental chaos. But, then I realized it was only two days, and those were in the depths of a gloomy winter. I pressed on, shared my cares with an empathizing friend, and realized the burden was lifting. It wasn't weeks or months; only a brief season. A season which I knew would come, but for which I was more prepared, largely because balanced thoughts told me the season would pass.

It is a more realistic approach to know there will times of darkness, and then to expect a season of refreshing. Whether a new Christian, or one conquering depression, if we revert to old thinking errors, we'll assume God has left us alone in the midst of our deep need.

Despite all our hopes, in the moments of disappointments, we may feel like the child in the morose Peggy Lee ballad, *Is That All There Is?* The lyrics darkly recall a child's anticipation of the circus. Remembering, as an adult, her bitter disappointment that the circus didn't live up to being the greatest show on earth, she asks, "Is that all there is?"

She answers, "Well, if that's all there is my friend, then let's keep dancing. Break out the booze and have a ball, if that's all there is!" The translation is, "If that's all there is, oh to hell with it! Just give up and endure the darkness."

This mindset condemns the emotionally ill to persistent failure and darkness. How can one assume where he is emotionally is not better than where he'd be without Jesus in his life? Through the years, when I wasn't following God's leading, He was there. When I thought life was too dark to endure, I did endure. How can I assume He did not work in the midst of those trials? Remember, He promised not to let me face more than I can endure, and I can endure far more than I thought. He was there all the time, protecting me from far worse. How can I dare say He was not meeting my deepest needs? Or, in times when I still suffer some darkness, that He is not meeting my needs still today?

How much darker might it be without His provision for healing? I must trust Him to continually renew my mind. I must learn to trust Him to help me be "content in whatever circumstances I am" (Philippians 4:11). As I press on to higher ground, I'll seek a godliness which "is a means of great gain when accompanied by contentment" (I Timothy 6:6).

Forgiveness – The Real Renewing

It is contentment which is so hard to attain. The biggest obstacle to contentment has been my lack of forgiveness. Until I could forgive, I could not cast aside the old mind.

The inability to forgive is a poison which infects the mind. "Not forgiving someone is like drinking poison yourself and expecting your enemy to die" (Shakespeare). Holding on to my poisoned and unforgiving mind, I could revive decades-old conflicts, reviving every negative emotion. Until I could forgive, the memories were a constant ingestion of poison. And, until I could forgive, I had to live within the pitiful irony of being unforgiving – the person who suffered the most was me.

Issues which I considered long past still remained. I had to learn forgiveness is more than passive acquiescence to pain; a decision to ignore and cover up old hurts. Covering up is not forgiveness; the hurts will surface again.

I could not forgive my son until I had also forgiven my abusive brother. Only after forgiving both of them could I accept Christ's forgiveness for me. Bitterness against another breeds bitterness against one's self. I could never move out of darkness without both forgiving others and accepting my forgiveness.

Forgiveness is hard to comprehend. It is not a learned skill, but is a result of other learning. It is not a hard science, but is a quality of character. Forgiveness is not only a decision of the mind, but a willingness of the heart. Forgiveness is not a fruit of the Spirit; it is a by-product of those ripening fruits.

Forgiveness is a facet of real, godly love - and is not achieved without a measure of that kind of love. We cannot begin to understand *agape* love if we aren't truly willing to forgive. Remembering Christ came to forgive, we will never be more like Christ than when we forgive.

More than Thoughts Alone

It sounds all neat and tidy now; overcoming depression by replacing a faulty set of thinking patterns with a new and improved set of thoughts. This appears to be exactly what I have written, but I must not let the appearance remain. The transition from darkness into His light, the renewing of the mind, cannot be reduced to a set of mental calisthenics; a fitness regimen based only upon logic. It cannot be reduced to only replacing one set of thinking patterns with another. Depending on renewed thinking alone limits the ways in which we accept the Spirit's working, reducing God's infinite wisdom to that which is fathomable by the finite wisdom of man.

It has been rightly said that what passes for depression today is the result of the lack of proper mental training. People with various emotional illnesses have done a great deal to train our minds to run a particular kind of race. To run as Christ would have us run, we must recondition our minds for a different kind of race; a race which we win by looking forward to the light rather than backwards toward the darkness.

There is vastly more to renewing the mind than simply daydreaming of Heaven, setting our thoughts on things above. There is vastly more to it than Pollyanna sweetness when the scripture tells us to set our thoughts upon "whatever is true, whatever is honorable, whatever is right, whatever is pure, whatever is lovely, whatever is of good repute…" Paul adds, "If there is any excellence and if anything of praise, dwell on these things (Philippians 4; 8-9). And, there is vastly more to it than simply pressing on to the prize. As Paul purposed, we must forget what is behind. Hanging onto the past and nurturing what is behind leaves little room for renewing the mind, for a more abundant today and for the promised Heaven tomorrow.

Yes, the continual renewing of the mind is vastly more than replacing one set of thoughts with another. While God knows my every need, even the smallest of them, I must never reduce Him to small matters; to mere patterns of thinking, or positive mental slogans. Reducing His working to thinking patterns seeks to make Him small. Most of all, it ignores the working of the Holy Spirit. More than thoughts, I must accept the Spirit's working in retraining me for the race God calls me to run. Old thoughts or new, I must get my spirit out of the way to let His Spirit have full sway. Seeking to understand His working in the renewing of the mind, I dare not ignore or minimize the working of the Holy Spirit.

I grew up in and still worship within a religious tradition which acknowledges the Holy Spirit, but largely functions without a top-of-mind awareness of its effect in our daily lives. When we are baptized for the remission of our sins, we receive a limited measure of the Holy Spirit which then resides in us. But, we seem to live as if He only resides there, not depending upon the Spirit to do much. Depending upon the power of the Word, we functionally negate the power of the Spirit.

The belief in a limited operation of the Spirit derives from depending upon God's words, more than His working in unknown ways. We hold to no scripted liturgy, but anyone who dares to swing very wide of the expected script is held in suspicion. A too-hardy "Amen" or "Hallelujah" is seemingly a bit too much. Relying on the Word is surer than relying upon an unknown work of the Spirit. Yet, within God's working through His Word, His Son, and His Spirit – there is a function and equilibrium of all three. Trusting in His "all things for good" means I trust the promises of God's Word, including the promise of the Spirit's encouragement, intercession and comforting.

Depending only upon the Word, some have essentially ignored the Spirit's role in their salvation from sin-ruled lives, and in their continuing need for conversion and regeneration. The reasoning seeks to constrain God to working within man's finite understanding of His words.

Seeking to understand the Spirit's working, I read words written in the present and active tenses. They tell me of a Spirit who is more than present in me; helping, testifying, comforting, strengthening, and interceding. However, some teach the Spirit does not work, but in almost the same breath proclaim the Spirit is a great help to us.

Avoiding the extremes, I cannot imagine a mindset given over to a charismatic reliance upon the Spirit manipulating my emotional strings like a mindless marionette. Neither will I reduce God's working to the black or red letters on a page.

As I am writing today, my wife and I are enjoying our last day at one of our favorite vacation places, the Oregon coast. From the loft of our house, I am looking out the windows at the waves and weather. It seems here I can also see the difference between depending only upon God's Word, and depending upon both His Word and His Spirit.

Back home, it doesn't take much to stir our urge for a trip to the coast. From only a picture we're ready to pack the car. From pictures I can tell you quite a bit about the coast. You can know there are beautiful sunsets, or violent storms. You can know about the rugged coastline, with forests descending to the shore. You can know about crashing waves, tide pools with otherworldly creatures, and the miles of lazy beaches.

But, looking at a picture is like looking through these windows. Stepping outside today makes all the difference in really *knowing* the coast. I feel the chill in the wind, and feel it whipping my collar. I feel the mist which is fogging my glasses. I see the squall swinging in from the south, and the squadron of pelicans skimming the waves, or diving like kamikaze. I hear the haughty cries of gulls, and see the sea lions floating lazily beyond the breakers. I hear the cadence and feel the concussion of crashing waves against the cliffs. I taste the salty spray. The experience is mesmerizing, and for an Oregon coast lover it is addicting.

Pictures alone are a poor substitute for the experience of being here; perhaps like depending only the Word while ignoring the Spirit. In the regeneration of my mind, I seek to depend on all His ways, both the revealed and the unknown. Avoiding either extreme, I'll depend on both to keep my reliance upon the other in check. Faith operates best when depending upon the Word and the Spirit. Faith thrives on both, even while lacking complete knowledge of either. I submit to the Word without complete knowledge of the Word. I will also submit to the Spirit without complete knowledge of the Spirit, while seeking to learn more God's ways. It has rightly been said, "One does not have to understand the working of the Spirit, simply trust the Spirit is working."

The result of renewing the mind by overcoming thinking errors and relying upon the God-given words of Truth, is a ripening of the Spirit's fruits – "love, joy, peace, patience, kindness, goodness, faithfulness" (Galatians 5:22). In all of my longing for light, the essential yearning is for the fruit of peace. I'm striving for peace which brings light to this life, shines light on my path towards the next life, and will be perfected in the bright light of His presence in that bright city.

I voice my longing for peace in this poem:

PERFECTED PEACE

Peace -
Quiet the chaos of my mind,
'til stillness in Him I find.
Peace -
Strength to climb the next hill,
still depending on His will.
Peace -
Through His Word, hear His voice,
though in trial still rejoice.

Peace -
By his sustaining power,
every day and every hour,
Peace –
Precious Balm of Gilead,
unto me, all He had.
Peace -
The will to walk another mile
by the light of His smile,
Peace -
To trust His nail-scarred hand,
the surest strength by which I stand.
Peace -
A full measure of His grace
'til I see His blessed face;
and
Perfected Peace -
That day I hear Him say,
"Well done, my child, come home to stay."

FIVE

GIVING VOICE

The transition from darkness into the light only happens when one's heart is softened and malleable in God's hands. Light comes when one purposes to conquer the darkness and cries out, "Create in me a clean heart, O, God, and renew a steadfast spirit within me" (Psalm 51:10).

Within a dark, sour heart, those words meant little to me. It was easy to presume that no one, not even God, knew how I felt. Surely, no one would understand. But, with a receptive heart, fertile ground ready to be planted for a new yield, the words availed much. They were my plea and, perhaps, the plea of others who seek the healing of their dark and broken spirits.

Despite a lifelong involvement in the church, consistently replacing old thinking patterns with renewed thoughts, thinking on whatever is pure, holy, and true, did not come easily. Conditioned to focus upon darkness and guilt, simply willing myself to think on higher and nobler things didn't make it so.

Frustrated by the chaos of my mind and aggravated by failures, I yearned to break the cycles of thinking which persistently brought darkness over me. It's still the reason for daily remembering, "I'm pressing on the upward way." Those words voiced my desire, but were insufficient to achieve the higher ground. Knowing much more was needed, I sought a deeper love of His Word.

The wonder of the Word is not from a head full of knowledge, but from a heart full of assurance, which leads me to desire more knowledge. The blessing is not yet in quoting the book, chapter, and verse of every truth, but in the confidence God fully knows my needs.

By His Word and Spirit, He is more than able to bring me from my darkness into His light.

As a brighter spiritual light was dawning, there were many situations which seemed like revelations. They were only new to me, for I then found the same truth within His Word. Truth was there all the time. I had not chosen to see it. And, God was there all the time – in darkness, I had not yet chosen to see Him.

I recall hearing on the radio someone saying, "If the light of the Word has grown dark in you, how deep is your darkness indeed." The words indicted me, and then I found their origin in the Word. This was proof not only to my lack of scriptural knowledge, but to my mental malaise.

"The eye is the lamp of the body. If your eyes are good, your whole body will be full of light. But if your eyes are bad, your whole body will be full of darkness. If then the light within you is darkness, how great is that darkness" (Matthew 6: 22-23)?

Those words convicted me; I couldn't get them out of my mind. The pursuit to higher ground must be within the True Light of His Word. The Word is the light and any other striving for light will be in vain. As one who heard the Word, but in darkness saw no light in it, I also lost my way back to the Light. Only the Word leads back to the True Light.

I cherish the story of Vincent Kituku, a friend from the Masai tribe of Kenya, which tells of finding one's way back home. Vincent tells about the traditions of the Masai at the impending death of a loved one. A person nearing death is carried to the top of a high hill and left there for their passing into the next life. A man, with the help of several others, carried his mother aloft on a stretcher up the lonely hill. Occasionally the men felt resistance, as if something was pulling against their progress. The resistance ceased for a time, but repeatedly something seemed to pull against them, and then let go.

After a fair distance, the man stopped to see what was pulling against their advance. He saw along the trail small clusters of leaves, pulled from the overhanging trees and dropped along the way. His frail mother had grasped the leaves and purposefully dropped them along the path. When asked why, she said she knew where home soon will be, but he would need the leaves to show him the way back to his home.

The mother was confident in her going home; she wanted her son to have confidence going to his home. Similarly, I needed a trail of leaves, the words of God, to show me the way back to the Light; to Jesus, "the way, the truth, and the [Light]." I didn't yet fully trust the trail to lead me home.

The transition from spiritual stagnation to vitality requires replacing old conversations with new ones. The "me, myself, and I" limits of my self-defeating and self-contained discourse had to be replaced. The new discourse requires two parties – God speaking to me, and me talking to Him.

There is always a conversation. The choice must be made – who is party to the conversation? It will either be God and me talking, or the Dark Angel and me talking. The one with whom I converse is the one directing my life. If I do not choose to talk to God, by default, the conversation is with the Dark Angel.

This Dark Angel is, of course, the devil. I've adopted the name for him because it more accurately describes him. He is the Prince of Darkness, leading me in my darkest days. He was an angel, who reminds me how far one can fall away from God.

I believe people have reduced their desire for God and Jesus, by first having reduced the existence and the nature of Satan. If Satan is not a Dark Angel working against the will of God, why is there any need for Jesus? The Dark Angel has been reduced to comedic standards. He's the red-horned character on humorous, greeting cards, or simply, the devil-made-me-do-it punch line to a joke. But, when our minds are totally unbalanced, held in such sway of chaotic thoughts that we can't focus on the Word of God, we dare not forget the suasion of the Dark Angel.

If we reduce the Dark Angel, we are trying to reduce the guilt of sin. If we can't be led by the Dark Angel, we rationalize we aren't very far away from Jesus. If the guilt of sin is lessened, then the need for Jesus is lessened. We do not see ourselves as missing the mark of righteousness. Minimizing both the Dark Angel and Jesus, we become spiritually negligent. We are vulnerable to the deceptions of sin, and hold only a vacuous kinship with the Father.

How did I remain involved in the church without an active conversation with God? Consistent Bible study and prayer were lacking in my life. There was little food to nourish the thoughts of "whatever is pure…" Spiritually, I was anorexic, existing on a starvation diet without His food and water for my soul.

I struggled for decades to fulfill my plans for my life. I nourished a chaotic mindset, a mix of highflying dreams and crashing frustrations for not having accomplished those dreams. I operated quietly on the outside. Inside, I was either emotionally vacant or viciously frantic. I was exhausted and living on the emotional edge. Finally, I had to let go of my plans, for their season had passed. I stopped striving for many wants, and became thankful for what I already have.

When I finally said, "Okay, God, I'll try it Your way," I didn't know completely to what I had committed. But, God used it as the beginning to turn me around, and in hindsight I can better explain, "Okay, God, I'll try it Your way."

Those words voiced the decision to submit my course to God's direction. The words were an earnest plead for His merciful healing, meaning, "God, I'm living way too close to the edge. Pull me back from the edge. Heal this wretched mind." When I finally prayed, "Pull me back from the edge," one foot was over the edge.

Several years ago amid a storm of stresses, I intentionally proclaimed me to be crazy. I purposely noted the date, and in years following remembered the date much like other anniversaries. It was an extreme absurdity, but it seemed easier to at least have one issue resolved. In the chaos of all-or-nothing thinking, I decided, "If I can't feel better than this, then I'll just be nuts and stop trying." Essentially, the decision was the commission of benign suicide. I was outwardly alive, but inwardly dead.

It was a variation of the mental escaping I practiced as a child. Amid the anxieties, it felt safer to escape by laughingly saying, "Paul, you *are* nuts. You always wondered what it would be like – well here you are!" The tragedy was by that age I should have grown to deal with adversity in healthier ways. I learned there truly was no escaping, for when I tried I carried my darkness and my sins with me.

The "crazy" mindset was from the depths of a spiritually destitute mind; a mind which could not live much longer without the breath of God. I had to let Him pull me back from the edge. He waited such a long time for me to come around to asking.

While I took so long to come around, I'm not alone. Moses went toe-to-toe with God, taking a long time to come around to God's plan. And Jonah's mind was slow to change, too; spending a few days in darkness. Both of them resisted God's plan for their lives. Like Moses and Jonah, God was working out His will in me. I could not see it all, but I saw just enough to desire the rest.

Submission to His will is more than giving up my will. Releasing control, (a continuing work in progress) is not throwing up my hands and quitting. Rather, it is opening my hand to take Jesus' hand. It is saying, "Okay, God, it is Your turn to lead. Lead me, Lord; show me Your way is better."

From this decision grew a deeper desire for knowing His Word. The desire grew not only from the Word itself, but in the ways I saw peoples' lives blessed by His Word. Through these people, I began to see more clearly the ways God works His will in us. The Word teaches and blesses those who seek Him, while it rebukes the hard-headed and defiant.

Some can accept God's Word without defiance, able to receive His simple, "I tell you the truth," direction for their lives. However, it is the other ways He teaches which convinces me of the Word's divine inspiration. It is the way the Bible meets peoples' needs in learning His will, or in overcoming their hardheadedness.

For those who find the Truth cold, Jesus paints the beautiful parables to plant a vision of Truth. For the defiant, Jesus reveals the price which must be paid by those who won't follow His Father's will. We see their hardships and sufferings for stubbornly resisting His way, or for partially following His will; a following which seeks to retain their control. We see their victories in submission, and their defeats in stubbornness.

I see myself in situations like those in which God had to overcome stubbornness and self-will. However, the dearest teachings to me come through the prayers of God's people – prayers intimate and passionate, grief-stricken and broken, or joyous in victory; heart and voice connected with the Father.

While in darkness, and depressed, I was not alone. Many in the Word were like me, and I'm blessed through the Word to hear their cries. Certainly, David's cries of distress in the Psalms are of one who despaired due to the deep gulf of trials before him.

"Save me, O God, for the waters have threatened my life. I have sunk in deep mire and there is no foothold; I have come into deep waters and a flood overflows me. O God, hasten to deliver me; O Lord, hasten to my help" (Psalm 69-70)

And, we rejoice as David exults, *"Shout joyfully to God, all the earth; sing the glory of His name; make His praise glorious. Say to God, 'How awesome are Your works!' All the earth will worship You, all will sing praises to You, they will sing praises to Your name" (Psalm 66:4).*

Clearly, David understood the transition from darkness into the Light. The lessons for me as I press on to higher ground, are also in David's words. As he prayed, so shall I.

"Hear my cry, O God; give heed to my prayer. From the end of the earth I call to You when my heart is faint; lead me to the Rock that is higher than I. You are my God; I will seek You earnestly; my soul thirsts for You, and my flesh yearns for You. In a dry and weary land where there is no water...my soul is satisfied. O God, in the greatness of Your lovingkindness, answer me with Your saving truth. Deliver me from the mire and do not let me sink. May the flood of deep waters not overflow me nor the deep swallow me up" (excerpts from Psalms 61, 63, and 69).

One of the first prayers I came to cherish is that of Hannah. She grieved for many years because of her barrenness. Though blessed in so many ways, her deep need and heaviest burden was for only one gift from God, a child. Year after year, greatly distressed, she prayed to the Lord and wept bitterly. She prayed specifically for a child.

I cannot say, like Hannah, I have only yearned for one blessing, nor did I persistently and fervently pray like her. But, the heaviest distress has been for the overcoming of depression. Year after year I've wanted to beat this darkness. My error was in not seeking to overcome the darkness following her example. I did not fervently pray with the same attitude. The true beauty of Hannah's prayers were not through her tears finding relief from her distress, but through her tears placing her whole trust in God.

I missed the contentment Hannah experienced even before she knew how bountifully God would answer her prayers. After praying, "Her face was no longer sad" (I Samuel 1:18). How much peace have I forfeited by not bringing my distress to the Lord? Ultimately, Hannah's prayers were answered in a measure far beyond what she had asked. How great His answer to me might have been had I prayed so many years ago? Only God can know!

The prayers of David, Hannah, and so many others, including Jesus, reveal a critical aspect of God's working – time. All things do work together for good, according to God's timing. David couches his prayers for deliverance in the words, "My prayer is to You, O Lord, at an acceptable time…" Hannah prayed for years, waiting for God's timing. And, Jesus spoke regarding His death on the cross, "in the fullness of time," or "the hour is come."

Many are the tragic outcomes of those who sought God's will but suffered greatly for not having waited on God's timing. Patience is not a common trait of human wisdom. We want an answer, and we want it now!

We sing a song about waiting on the Lord's timing, but it's questionable how good we are at following its words;

> *Teach me Lord to wait down on my knees,*
> *'til in Your own good time you answer my pleas*
> *Teach me not to rely on what others may do,*
> *But to wait in prayer for an answer from You.*

Those who wait upon the Lord shall renew their strength
They shall mount up with wings like eagles,
They shall run and not grow weary,
They shall walk and not faint,
Teach me Lord, teach me Lord to wait.

We sing the words far better than we live the message. In essence we're saying, "Lord, we trust You for an answer, but can't You make it quick?" We want it quickly; God promises "steadfast and sure". His ways are above our ways, including His timing.

We're trained to make it quick and to want it quicker; a major cause of our anxieties. Television marketers in the wee hours of the morning know our anxieties, including time. An advertising acronym for their pitches is FUD – short for "fears, uncertainties and doubts". Likely, if you're watching TV at three in the morning, you are worried about something. If not, the pitchmen will create a worry from your F's, U's, or D's.

If you're too fat, too ugly, too poor, and too powerless, just the right pill, the right makeup, the right business scheme, or self-help course will fix your woes. And, do it right now! And, as an added bonus, they say, "This is a limited offer…" In other words, "Do it now and beat everyone else to the prize. All will be well, and all people will admire your success!" Sadly, of the many "ways which seem right unto man" (Proverbs 14:12), there are essentially two – speed and greed.

David, in Psalm 30, understood God's timing, writing:

"Out of the depths, I have cried out to You, O Lord. Lord, hear my voice! Let Your ear be attentive to the voice of my supplications… I wait for the Lord, my soul does wait, and in His Word I do hope. My soul waits for the Lord more than the watchman for the morning; indeed more than the watchman waits for the morning." Yes, he watches as if the answer will come in the morning, but his "soul does wait."

It has been said, if it seems the Lord has said "No," it is because

He will have a greater "Yes." Sometimes "No" really means "Wait." Wait for the Lord's greater "Yes."

A beautiful example of waiting for His "Yes" is Hannah. Though she suffered heavily for her barrenness, it is a testimony of her faithful waiting. Every tormented year must have seemed to be a "No." Even with her deep faith, we can imagine Hannah thinking, "Lord, make it quick. I've had enough of this other wife's boasting!" But, in the Lord's timing, His greater "Yes" came in the blessing of Samuel. And, because she honored her vow to dedicate Samuel to the Lord, He blessed Hannah with five more children, making a six-fold, "Yes!"

Striving to accomplish my plans, I've fought mightily over timing, though I should have known better. Many years ago, concerning an issue for which I expected a quick answer, I asked a friend to fast and pray with me. Though it was a time in my life when I didn't consistently depend on prayer, the fasting centered my thoughts on the desires of my heart. Today, I can't recall the exact words I prayed, but I can recall the exact answer. "You expect everything to come too fast. When it is time, you'll know the answer." It took years to understand the answer, and truthfully, I had long since forgotten it. Yet, now as I seek God's ways, He reminds me to, "Wait for My "Yes." This does not mean God is withholding His blessings. It means I am not ready to receive them.

I created chaos by trying to force my plans, and to force them to fit my timing. I am much like the story of a man who found a cocoon of a butterfly. One day an opening appeared in the cocoon. The man watched for several hours as the butterfly struggled to force its way through the little hole. Seemingly it had gone as far as it could, and would never fly freely.

With a pair of scissors, the man sought to help the butterfly by snipping away the remaining cocoon. The butterfly emerged, but its body was swollen and its wings were small and shriveled. The man expected the wings to unfold and expand to support the body, which would contract in time. Neither happened; the butterfly never flew. It spent its life crawling, with a swollen body and shriveled wings. The man did not know the restricting cocoon and the struggle to escape were necessary. It was God's way of forcing fluid from the butterfly's body into its wings.

The parallel in my life is in forcing my plans for which I was not fully prepared. By submitting to seek God's way, I was also saying, "Okay, I'll also follow Your timing." In following His timing, and His Word, He is preparing me for "flight."

Without His Word there is no way for me to follow His will. Trying to follow His course, I had to "hear" His voice in the only way we can – by "giving voice" to His Word. Many times I've sung, "Why from the sunshine of love will thou roam… Jesus is calling today," He is calling, but I will only know the calling to "the sunshine of love" by hearing His voice.

While desiring peace, I began to see the conflict between what we desire and how we seek to find it. Ironically, we yearn for peace, yet feed on strife. We yearn for wisdom yet revel in foolishness. We yearn for His Spirit, yet thrill in the flesh.

God does not cast His choicest pearls of blessings until we reconcile our actions with our yearnings. Granting wisdom to one who delights in foolishness is like casting His pearls into the barrow pit. Granting His sweet peace to one who sows discord produces no gain. And, His Spirit will not remain in the heart of one which makes provision for the flesh.

The Spirit indwells hearts which have made accomodation for its dwelling. To receive His peace, His wisdom and His Spirit, I must prepare a place in my heart. Preparation is made through giving voice to His Word and to prayer. Only then will my heart be receptive. Only then will the Spirit thrive within me.

When I first turned back to His Word, the motivation was not for an assurance of my faith, but for peace. But, God can use any motivation which brings one to His Word. In the turbulent days following my son's crimes, my heart was broken. I had to find peace from worrying that my failure as a father led to my son's failures. I was burdened by remembering just a bit of scripture about the sins of the father visiting upon their children. "The Lord, the Lord God, compassionate and gracious, slow to anger, and abounding in lovingkindness and truth; who keeps lovingkindness for thousands, who forgives iniquity, transgression and sin; yet He will by no means leave the guilty unpunished, *visiting the iniquities of the father upon the children* and on the grandchildren to the third and fourth generations" (Exodus 34:6-7). Did this mean my sin provoked the son to sin, as a consequence of my sin?

I was chilled by the question. I understood being accountable for my wrongs, but would I in judgment be accountable for his wrongs, or he for mine? I was compelled to place the blame somewhere. I sought someone to blame, for someone must have twisted my son's life. (Indeed, someone had.) While any honest father can look back and see how he could have done better, this anxiety went further. I feared that I was responsible for his sin.

It took a long time to accept the answer, and the meaning of the verse, "The father's sins are visited upon the children." It is not the father's sins causing the son to sin, but the consequences of a father's sin may affect his children. We see children who suffer the effects of their parent's failures for generations to come. Indeed, we suffer from the sin of Adam; its consequences visiting upon untold numbers of generations. Our children may endure the consequences of our sins, but each must answer for his own transgressions. Through Ezekiel 18:20-21, I began to settle my mind. I know my son can be redeemed from the penalty of his sins, and me as well.

"The person who sins will die. The son will not bear the punishment for the father's iniquity, nor will the father bear the punishment for the son's iniquity; the righteousness of the righteous will be upon himself and the wickedness of the wicked will be upon himself. But, if the wicked man turns from all his sins which he has committed and observes all My statutes and practices justice and righteousness, he shall surely live; he shall not die."

While we are born without sin, we are born prone to sin. Since the fall of Adam, sin has burdened every generation. Each person is vulnerable to and succumbs to different temptations. Whatever the nature of one's sin, the challenge is the same – we must die to sin.

"Brethren, we are under obligation, not to the flesh, to live according to the flesh – for if you live according to the flesh, you must die; but if by the Spirit you are putting to death the deeds of the body, you will live" (Romans 8:12-13).

Nothing I did led to my son's sin; rather, it is due to what I did not do. My sins of omission contributed to his lack of spiritual defenses against the temptations to sin. How much different might the course of his life be today if he'd seen me consistently being the spiritual father and leader I'm called to be? If in the trials of my life my son had seen me turn to Jesus and the Word, he may have developed the spiritual skills to overcome his temptations to sin. By my omissions I am responsible to a degree, but for that, too, there is forgiveness.

In the anxious days of raising both my sons, I wasn't the real man of God they needed. I often felt the frustrations of not knowing how to love them as needed. The misgivings haunt me as in the words of the story, *A River Runs Through It.* The father, a minister dealing with the beating death of his prodigal son, wrestles with his inability to love, or to give of himself as the son needed.

"Each one of us here today will at one time in our lives look upon a loved one and ask the same question. We are willing to help, Lord, but what if anything is needed? For it is true we can seldom help those closest to us. Either we don't know what part of ourselves to give, or more often than not, the part we have to give is not wanted. And so, it is those we live with and should know who elude us, but we can still love them. We can love completely without complete understanding."

It seems the part I had to give my sons was not wanted. As children or parents, we do not get a do-over. I pray contrition, a doubled portion of love, and living in the suasion of God, now bridges my failures of the past.

Through the confusions and frustrations of guilt, the Dark Angel can gain a foothold in our lives. If one has not purposed to maintain a spiritually, life-sustaining conversation with God, the Dark Angel will hold us in his deep darkness.

Real peace requires both sides of the conversation. I could hear His voice through the Word; He also wants to hear my voice. To know peace and find His light, God waited to hear through my prayers that I believe, "Truly I say to you, if you have faith and do not doubt...all things you ask in prayer, believing, you will receive" (Matthew 21: 21-22). This had been another verse which seemed too much like Pollyanna. In darkness, and a self-starved faith, I had never trusted this promise. Much like the effort required to think upon, "whatever is pure, whatever is true," I had to work towards developing a heart to pray.

The effort reminds me of a sales guru's quote, "Concentrated thoughts produce desired results." As a quote, it is hardly a head turner; doubtful those words will ever be on a bumper sticker. Yet, the reasoning is valid. In biblical terms, it translates, "For as he thinks within himself, so he is" (Proverbs 23:7).

As one just beginning "concentrated thoughts" voiced in prayer to God, those verses assured me of God's provision. Troubling though is the one phrase, "and do not doubt" (Matthew 12:21). Doubt is the broken hinge on the gateway to answered prayer. Without a habit of fervent prayer, doubt is a high hurdle.

With almost as much consistency as beginning each day with, "I'm pressing on the upward way," I began to pray. Often, it was hard to trust God was hearing me. It was hard to maintain concentration. Doubt was almost always near. Often the foremost matter of prayer was, "I do believe; help my unbelief" (Mark 9:24). The conflict between belief and unbelief was proof of the inadequacy of my conversations with God. Doubt was proof of my long-starved faith.

When the desire to pray was conflicted with my inadequacy in praying, I depended upon the song, *I Need Thee Every Hour.*

I need Thee every hour,
Most gracious Lord;
No tender voice like Thine,
Can peace afford.

I need Thee every hour,
Stay Thou nearby;
Temptations lose their power,
When Thou art nigh.

I need thee, O, I need Thee,
Every hour I need Thee!
O bless me now my Savior,
I come to Thee.

As the Lord had done all through the years, the words of songs were the trusted tether. They bore my prayers as I sought His working in my life. Still, I began to see again that I wanted an answer for every care too quickly. My mindset remained too close to the demand to, "Make it quick, Lord. "

The yearning to draw close to God through prayer was founded in a prayer experience from ten years ago. At the time, the experience was jarringly foreign to my mindset of proper prayer. Sadly, it is not an overstatement to admit to a measure of revulsion.

In the shock of a family tragedy I called my brother, Ben. While we were essentially estranged by the distance of miles misunderstandings, I knew he held a vibrant faith in the power of fervent prayer. I trusted him to pray when it seemed I could not.

My expectations in asking him to pray proved very different from his response. I tentatively meant, "Oh, if you will, if you remember, perhaps when you pray before a meal, please pray about my son." However, within the scope of my brother's prayer life, he heard, "The effective prayer of a righteous man can accomplish much" (James 5:16). While on the phone, he launched into a prayer like none I'd ever experienced. Yet, my brother's assurance of God's answer was palpable; claiming victory through Jesus' intercession.

I was stunned by his prayer nearly as much as by the tragedy. The tenor of his prayer was unlike anything of mine. I struggled to understand it, until I came to understand my prayer voice doesn't need to be like his. His assurance didn't derive from the form of his prayer, but from his steadfastness in prayer. My prayer voice likely will never be like my brother's. I'm not called to be an imitator of him, but an imitator of Christ. My prayers derive from my relationship with Christ, and from my words.

My growing purpose in prayer began also within the context of striving to pursue a second-half-of-life career change. The issue was consuming nearly all of my energy, and daily ratcheted up anxieties. I could not force my plans to fruition.

Already, the Spirit was converting the focus from my plans to God's plans. The roadblocks I faced were changing my willingness to accept the mindset of David. I began to trust,

"The eyes of the Lord are toward the righteous, and His ears are open to their cry. The righteous cry and the Lord hears and delivers them out of their troubles. The Lord is near to the brokenhearted and saves those who are crushed in spirit" (Psalm 34).

From within my imbalanced mind, the pressing for career change, and the tragedy of my son's life, I first voiced the words, "Okay, God, I'll try it Your way." It was then with greater fervor I began to pray, and to strive towards thinking on "whatever is pure." Still, I wrestled with knowing just which way to turn. Though the salve to my spirit did not heal quickly, I was certain of its healing.

As struggles persisted, particularly with my career, I knew a breaking point was imminent. I was walking way too close to the emotional edge. One morning while walking across the parking lot at work, I literally called out, "God, I need answer; give me something to pursue!" And, just as promised, His ears were open to my cry. That very day an answer came.

In those times when I prayed, "Lord, sort out the chaos, I need an answer," He answered. There would often be a situation to which I could apply the goal of thinking "whatever is pure." Then, without knowing exactly when the prayer was answered, the chaos cleared. I suspect the answer came as soon as I turned my thoughts towards whatever is pure.

In the coming weeks this experience occurred several times. Every time I cried out, the answer came – every time. God was proving the

Spirit's working in all things for good hinges upon a confirmation of my faith through prayer. This growing reliance upon "giving voice" was teaching me this valuable truth – the Word is the builder of faith; prayer is the confirmation of faith. The immediate value was a growing lightness of my spirit in peace.

I began to realize another change. There were fewer days when I had to remind myself of the admonition, "and do not doubt." The doubt was being overcome by words such as Romans 8:18-25.

"I consider that the sufferings of this present time are not worthy to be compared with the glory that is to be revealed to us. For the anxious longing of the creation waits eagerly for the revealing of the sons of God. For the creation was subjected to futility, not willingly, but because of Him who subjected it, in hope that the creation itself also will be set free from its slavery to corruption and into the freedom of the glory of the children of God. For we know that the whole creation groans and suffers the pain of childbirth together until now. And not only this, but also we ourselves, having the first fruits of the Spirit, even we groan within ourselves, waiting eagerly for our adoption as sons, the redemption of the body. For in hope we have been saved, but hope that is seen is not hope; for who hopes for what he already sees? But, if we hope for what we do not see, with perseverance we wait eagerly for it."

Those words brought light to me, helping me overcome the doubts. They added to my confidence that the dangerously dark days are past. The words *anxious longing, waiting eagerly, groan, hope,* and *perseverance,* produced an earnest expectation through prayer. More often now, my prayers are voiced in the mindset of earnest expectation.

From the beginning, I asked, "What transpires in one's life to make him step out, to change from marking time to marching onward?" The answer, simpler than the introspection, is this. By confidence in the Spirit's working in all things for good, I have found an *earnest expectation* of Light, and a hopeful future in this life and in the promised glory of Heaven to come. Just as light overwhelms darkness; an earnest expectation overwhelms doubt.

Recently though, I received a troubling reminder of my life prior to depending upon prayer. It helped me remember my dependence upon calling out to God, is a matter of daily calling out to Him. Like the manna God provided for the Israelites, they needed a fresh provision each day. Yesterday's manna only met their need for yesterday, and today's manna only meets today's need. As a person learning to be dependent upon God's working through prayer, there is a daily need for a fresh provision, manna to my soul, and fresh nourishment to my faith.

I had been spiritually riding high, enjoying a deeper faith, and a deeper conviction of my purpose. I was experiencing a confident kinship with Christ, and a rare boldness to speak out about God's working. I was living amid wonderfully rich, then-sings-my-soul days.

However, the next day my spirit was troubled. Early, while driving to work, I was already relying on the words, "I'll not be moved, I'll not be moved from Mt. Zion. My faith is anchored there and it shall stand." I was anxious about unknown and assumed challenges of the day. I purposely altered my routine to work alone that day, avoiding interactions as much as possible. I was trying to escape and I recognized some extreme thoughts were developing. I kept relying on the words, "I'm pressing on the upward way," to trip the cycle of negative thoughts. I tried to dwell on whatever is pure, holy, and true.

I earnestly tried to "not be moved." But I failed, feeling like a porcupine ready to throw my quills into anyone. I broke my faith, sinned, and spoke in ways for which I was ashamed, and Jesus was sorrowful. I was operating within my old mindset. I knew I was failing, but couldn't get a handle on it.

I remember thinking, "I've got to get this chaos out of my mind!" Then I recognized the problem. I had only done everything I could do to settle the chaos, without calling out to God. I was depending only on my will to renew my thoughts, and taking the reins of my life out of Jesus' grip. I knew that every time I called out to God the healing was granted. But, when I forgot to pray, it was a miserable day without His manna for my soul. Oh, how I know now the "pressing on to the prize for which I have been called," requires a daily pressing on in prayer.

I suspect it was a similar withdrawal from prayer which led to a recent dark period for my imprisoned son. He, too, had been riding spiritually high, despite the violent darkness of prison. But, in recent letters, there were signs of regression, signs he was struggling. Maybe it was an all-or-nothing thinking error which made him believe his darkness was all past. More than likely, it was simply the rancid darkness within the prison walls.

We received a letter which confirmed his struggles; a letter which felt like another shoe dropping. It wasn't a big "shoe," and turned into an opportunity to remember, "For as a man thinks within himself, so he is" (Proverbs 23:7). My son, again, was struggling against his thoughts, becoming those thoughts in action.

The scripture is simple, straightforward and true, "For *as* a man thinks within himself, so he is." It seems simple, but there is more to it. The *as* can mean *how* or *what* he thinks, he is. The desire of one's heart may be for righteousness, but his thoughts still hinge on what he *hates*. In the duplicity of wills, the thoughts in *hate* overwhelm the desire for good.

I believe my son never wanted to sin as he has. By his spirit and innate sensitivity I know the basic desires of his heart were for good. However, his desires were subverted by hatred for that which he did not want to be. In dwelling on what he hated, he became what he loathed.

He struggled as the Apostle Paul struggled, "That I do not want to do, I do." The key, as Paul knew, is forgetting what is behind and pressing on to the future. Living in our past, while desiring to do what is good, condemns us to repeat the past.

I struggled with the same faulty thinking. While desiring what is good, but dwelling on what I hated, I often became what I hated. Just as out of the stores of our hearts our tongue speaks, out of the stores of our hearts we sin. A heart which stores up hate, and a mind which dwells in hate, will only yield hateful sin. One cannot think on whatever is pure while clinging to whatever is foul.

For my son and for me, our daily prayer must include a plea to "create a clean heart in me, O, God, and renew a steadfast spirit within me" (Psalm 51:10). It must include thanksgiving for the promise yesterday's sins are forgiven and a commitment to slip the reins on our lives back into Jesus' hands. The prayer is,

"Heavenly Father, by your grace shed like the blood of Your Son for my redemption, I thank You for knowing the guilt of yesterday's sins is past and forgotten. By the Spirit, help me to forget my guilt also, as I depend upon You to create a clean heart in me, O, God, and to renew a steadfast spirit within me. Father, You know I struggle to release the past and live for the present, as I continue to seek the future prize of Heaven. Help me to know the presence of Your ever-effective Love. Help me to release control of my life, trusting more fully in Jesus, as I slip the reins back into His hands. Help me to ever seek the True Way by following Christ's leading, trusting also his intercession for this prayer unto You, my God." Amen.

In the mindset of this prayer, I came to realize those who truly seek Him are always beggars before the Lord. In a sense, we are like the crippled beggar at the temple gate.

How can I think such a thing when through Christ we are to be more than conquerors? Where is the victory in Christ if we are still lowly beggars? God has blessed us so richly; even the poor among us are rich. He gave His Son for us, investing the matchless worth of Jesus for our sins. So, how are we lowly beggars?

I don't see the beggar at the temple gate as such a pitiful soul. He knows where to find aid. He knows that while most of the world pretends to see no need among them, at the temple gate there are alms. The beggar knows his source. May we, also, like the beggar know our Source; know the One who is our strength, our sword, our shield, and our deliverer. Then we, even as beggars, will surely be the conquerors!

The essential, soul-felt need which motivates anyone to a vital conversation with God is simply to feel He is near. When we're unsure of our course, particularly in times of stress, transition, or darkness, we long to know He is near. We are told to, in some ways, remain as a little child. The scriptural call to enter the kingdom of Heaven as a child is the call to live in wonder, eagerness, and the optimism of living for Jesus. It is the call to be submissive, accepting, and secure in the Word of God.

Can there be anything dearer or more intriguing than a little child so full of wonder, so eager for new experiences, and so full of optimism? Even dearer, is the beauty of a child sure of his security in the guiding hand of a loved one?

I saw a little boy walking along the top of a narrow, waist-high wall. He was walking in the staccato steps of a toddler, but not at all timid about walking atop the wall. He did not hold out his arms for balance, or in anticipation that he might fall. He walked fearlessly. Yet, his security was not his own. The little boy was secured by his father's hand upon his shoulder. The child was eager to trust his father, confident in his touch.

As we step into the transitions of our lives, we yearn for confidence we will not fall. We, like the little boy, yearn for the security of knowing God's hand is on our shoulder. Spiritually, we may be stepping along a narrow wall. We want to know our Father walks beside us. As in the words of this poem, each of us wants to feel, *His Hand Upon My Shoulder.*

Like my Mother's soothing touch,
to calm my inward tears;
is His hand upon my shoulder,
comforting, through all the years.

He bids my anxious heart confess,
all my cares on Him to lay;
And, His hand upon my shoulder,
calls me more 'oft to pray.

My thoughts and steps may wander,
far wide of the narrow gate;
yet, His hand upon my shoulder,
again, my way makes straight.

When I know not where to turn,
and, for only peace I yearn;
with His hand upon my shoulder,
more of His love I learn.

"Lo, I am with you always",
ne'er forget that "I Am" here;
for His hand upon my shoulder,
stills my oft' uncertain fear.

Likely when much older,
yet, maybe long before,
by His hand upon my shoulder,
He will lead to Heaven's shore.

I know His hand is on my shoulder; His Word tells me so. By faith through prayer, I confirm His hand is there. In the present light, I revel in His security. Pressing on to higher ground and to the prize of Heaven, I trust His hand will lead me there. What other reason could I need for giving voice?

SIX

VESTED IN TRUTH

The spiritual benefit of renewing the mind is gaining a fertile mind, receptive to a fresh planting of truth; the Truth, with a capital "T". Within the cycles of depressive thoughts, it is impossible to see Truth. If seen, it is not openly and objectively received. At best, through the distorted lens of thinking errors, Truth is only faintly seen, as through a dark veil. Truth not clearly seen is still Truth, but it is diminished in its efficacy to change, direct, and sustain life.

In overcoming depression, the striving is for light, and ultimately, for the powerful light of Jesus. One who desires to become more like Christ must seek to dwell in His light. To be more like Him, we must become invested in His Word until we are wholly vested in Truth, resulting in a steadfast faith and light.

We usually consider the word *vested* in regards to financial matters – usually profit sharing or pension plans. The theory portends that after a prescribed period of time, once we've invested ourselves into a job, we are vested; meaning there is an amount of money which is held in irrevocable trust for our benefit. At least in theory, the money is ours and cannot be lost. We are vested.

About the time I earnestly began to overcome my darkness, I heard a man claim his faith never waivers. He avowed, no matter what comes his way, his faith is constant and certain. Hearing him, and assessing his life and demeanor through my darkly-colored lenses, I was doubtful of his claim. More than doubtful, I scoffed, "Man, you have to be kidding! How arrogant can you get?"

Rather than doubting him, I soon decided I wanted the same confidence in my faith, assuming, "Well, if he can have it, I can, too!" I purposed to become so invested in the Word that whatever may come my way, my faith will be certain.

For those who have known me well or long, they'll also know a steadfast, immovable faith has not been mine. There have been storms which unsettled my faith; some which I should have weathered on a surer foundation than I had built.

The same people will recall others we thought were solidly grounded in their faith, but who fell away, or let themselves be led astray. Sometimes it was highly esteemed preacher or elder drawn away by an ill wind of false doctrine, or by pride born from self-perceived higher wisdom. Sometimes it is a long-time Christian led away by a second marriage to an unbeliever. Often, it's the person who wonders, "What's in it for me?" Either way, they lose their investment. Their irrevocable trust is forfeited by lack of their continual investment in their faith.

We are called to be steadfast and immovable in our faith, by a growing knowledge of the Word and by the Spirit's working through the Word to instruct us. Becoming vested in Truth, and vested in an irrevocable faith, is to become more like the Apostle Paul. Certainly, Paul was one who invested himself into the purposes of God, holding a faith which could not be moved.

I return again to Paul because I see so much which could lead him into a darkly, depressive mindset. If Paul was not wholly vested in Truth and wholly focused upon Christ's calling, he could have been a maniac; perhaps with justifiable cause.

Paul reveals his intense and fallible humanity. We see his frustrations, his sarcasm-veiled anger, and his burdened soul. Concerning the hardships he suffered, he wrote, "We were under great pressure far beyond our ability to endure, so that we despaired even of life. Indeed, in our hearts we felt the sentence of death" (I Corinthians 1:8-9). The same Paul who could rejoice while bound in prison chains also despaired to "the sentence of death."

Paul's thoughts swung widely to the extremes, which is not surprising of a man who lived in all ways to the extreme. As Saul persecuting the Christians, or as Paul striving to establish the Lord's church, he was an all-or-nothing man. Paul is never lukewarm.

Paul was frustrated by the churches of Corinth, Ephesus, and Galatia. Having ministered and established those churches, Judaizing teachers and idolaters moved in to compromise and corrupt the church. Paul again had to instruct them in the better way of the new covenant. Frustrated, he resorted to name calling, labeling the Judaizers as dogs. "Watch out for dogs, those men who do evil, those mutilators of the flesh." ("Flesh" referring to the "Word becomes flesh".) They were dogs, as in the "dogs who return to eat their own vomit" (II Peter 2:22). They were dogs who longed to feast not on the pure Truth, but sought to corrupt the New Feast with the Old Law.

Paul revealed his weakness towards extreme thoughts as he dealt with the Israelites in II Corinthians 11. Justifying his ministry, Paul's thinking veered to the extreme. He had a belly full of them! He was angry enough to spit! He writes,

"Are they servants of Christ - I speak as if insane – I more so; in far more labors, in far more imprisonments, beaten time without number, often in danger of death. Five times I received from the Jews thirty-nine lashes. Three times I was beaten with rods, once I was stoned; three times I was shipwrecked, a night and a day I have spent in the deep. I have been on frequent journeys, in danger from rivers, in dangers from robbers, dangers from my countrymen, danger from the Gentiles, dangers in the city, dangers in the wilderness, dangers on the sea, dangers among the brethren; I have been in labor and hardship many sleepless nights, in hunger and thirst, often without food in cold and exposure. Apart from such external things, there is the daily pressure on me of concern for all the churches" (v. 23-28).

Clearly, in the many dangers Paul endured, he lived in the extreme. It is easy to understand why he was given to bouts of extreme thinking – despair, fear, and labeling. But, the power of Paul's story is in knowing while his thinking veered to the extremes he never, even for a moment, forfeited his faith. He never lost his investment in Truth. He remained wholly vested in the mission.

Paul understood the new converts were not sufficiently vested in Truth, leaving them vulnerable to losing their new faith. Thus, he continued writing to them, or sent his fellow workers to "reprove, rebuke, and exhort" them "in the way of God more perfectly" (I Timothy 4:2; Acts 18:26).

Paul's mind was renewed and balanced by his calling in Christ's purposes. The proof of Paul's investment in Truth was not in enduring hardships and dangers. The proof of his investment is in his words, "Apart from external things, there is the daily pressure on me of concern for all the churches." The words defined his focus, proved his calling and reproved his mindset. Paul's steadfast devotion to his mission as a soldier of the cross balanced and sustained him. Christ's mission was Paul's center of gravity. I believe Paul had to endure his "thorn in the flesh" as a result of his tendency towards thinking in the extreme. It was his thorn which reminded Paul to renew and rebalance his mindset. The thorn reminded him of the central cause of his life. The thorn reminded him daily by Whom he was called.

As I pursue higher ground, I strive more like Christ by striving to be more like Paul. In my past mindset, shackled by rampant thinking errors, I often remained in the extreme. If, like Paul, I had learned of the problems developing in the churches he'd established, my old thinking patterns would have locked in gear. I'd assume, "Now it's just *all* a big mess. (Assuming, all-or-nothing thinking, and catastrophizing) Or, I'd think, "It'll never work; to hell with all of them!" (That's *all* the thinking errors at once.) Either thought would be from a mind dissuaded and frustrated; a mind not vested in Truth. The Apostle Paul, *far* wiser than me, just shook the dust off his feet and pressed on "to the prize for which (he) was called heavenward in Christ Jesus." Paul, past all dangers of his circumstances and all frustrations in his mission could, like the song, say, "I'll not be moved!"

> *I cried out to Jesus and He answered;*
> *I waited patiently and He came.*
> *He brought me from the darkest valley,*
> *And set me on a solid rock where I'll stay.*

The love that I found, it never ceases'
'cause it fills me brand new everyday.
And His thoughts are always upon me,
Then I shall stand no matter what comes my way.

I'll not be moved, I'll not be moved from Mt. Zion.
My faith is anchored there and it shall hold.
He's my tower to lean on, my fortress where I can hide.
I'll not be moved, I'll not be moved from Mt. Zion.

Truth – oh my, just the single word stirs debate. Add the redundant word "absolute," and many folks will grind their teeth. Many believe there is nothing absolute about truth, contending God would not inhibit the mind of His highest creation, by imposing anything absolute. Many others don't believe we can comprehend, or ever agree, about what is true. Many will claim an adherence to Truth is not important, saying, "There is grace, so why does it really matter?" The small remainder, including me, hold to a conviction in irrefutable, inerrant, and God-ordained Truth; Truth which itself is a manifestation of God. "In the beginning was the Word, and the Word was God" (John 1:1).

In our pluralistic culture truth is relative, volatile, and transient. Truth is defined for personal gain. One's truth is as valid as the next. In this relativistic approach to small "t" truth, everyone's truth is good enough, but unique. However, living within the purposes of God requires the submission of individual truth to the higher wisdom of His capital "T" Truth.

Truth does not negate the truth about one's life. There is, indeed, a true story about each one of us, but the experiences by which we define our lives must never become the definition of Truth. We can have our own small "t" truth, if it is overwhelmed by capital "T" Truth.

The danger of one's own truth is it may be based upon faulty assumptions and conclusions. One's truth, cooked in the stew of errant human logic and emotional responses to the past, can be a toxic brew of self-limiting lies. One's truth created subjectively in response to crises or personal lusts, may hold no truth at all. My transition from darkness to light is really the subjugation of my truth to His Truth; when His Truth overwhelmed mine.

One may argue we cannot know the Truth – so many translations, paraphrases, and alleged contradictions; so many warring doctrines, with every preacher proclaiming his words are true. Too often the preacher is a chef, tweaking the recipe of truth to suit his personal taste. Some bake a sweet, tender loaf of love and grace; others serve only a vengeful porridge of hot wrath and judgment. Both recipes vary with the tastes of the times; some with no higher purpose than to be politically palatable or financially profitable. Both recipes are putrid concoctions which God abhors.

Still, I trust we can know the Truth. Beyond all faulty mindsets, all errant motivations, all the twists of mans' logic, we have the Word in its original language which never changes according to the tastes of the times. To know Truth is to know only the words which have never changed.

There is societal pressure, and sadly pressure within the church, to deny Truth; to decry Truth which some see as a tool of dogmatic theocracy. Perhaps, for good reason, when adherence to dogma is demanded in the absence of real love. But, the call to abandon dogma is often a ruse for elevating man's wisdom. Truth with an admixture of man's wisdom becomes a sullied investment, separating us from the love of God, for if we do not love His Truth, we truly do not love Him. Submission to Truth requires accepting every, "Thus sayeth the Lord," and every, "I tell you the truth."

Capital "T" Truth is resisted because it is an abstraction, beyond the conceptions of mans' thinking. Understanding Truth in the abstract is akin to a person, blind since birth, understanding light and sight. Within every experience of a blind person there is no reference for sight. Truth, like light, must be seen to be understood. God in His wisdom foreknew this.

God also knew man's mindset is highly prone towards doubt. Like the Apostle, Thomas, who would not believe Jesus' resurrection until he touched the nail-scarred hands, it is hard to accept absolute Truth without seeing it. Thomas, like a blind person, by his experiences had no spiritual sight to accept Christ's resurrection. Truth had to be fleshed out in the hands of Christ before Thomas would invest his faith.

Absolute Truth was seen in the flesh. God ordained Truth to be fleshed out in the Son of Man, Jesus Christ. The words of the apostles and prophets are our eyes to see Him.

Consider the pattern of italicized words, beginning in John 17:17. As part of Christ's intimate prayer to His Father, He says, "Sanctify them in truth, Your *word* is *truth.*" In John 1:14, we read, "And the *word* became *flesh,* and dwelt among us, and we *saw* His glory, glory as the only begotten from the Father, full of grace and *truth.*" And, consider the words of Acts 17:28, "In Him, (*Him* being a manifestation of *Truth*) we *live* and *move* and *exist.*"

God knew full well His Word must be seen in flesh, in His Son, to be understood. If, "Thy word is truth," if the "Word became flesh," and if Jesus lives today, then Truth is incarnate, sentient, and breathing. Truth breathes! And, if God, the Word, and Truth are one, Acts 17:28 can well be worded, "In Truth, we live and move and *breathe.*" The Truth in which we live, move and breathe is the same Truth I intend to invest, until I am wholly vested in Truth.

In the wisdom of God, Truth and Grace work together in the nail-scarred hands of Jesus. Yet, in the mind of sinful man, Truth and Grace are warring abstractions. Minimizing Truth requires expanding God's Grace, but Grace alone negates Truth. We depend upon both, for in both is the fullness of God's plan.

Since I was a little boy I wonder how many times I heard, "the Word became flesh." Perhaps, a preacher has followed the same scriptures to teach the authority of God's Word as Truth. But, finally in pressing on to higher ground, "the Word became flesh" really means something. It is the source of the bright light overcoming my darkness.

In the biblical accounts of miracles, The Word becoming flesh is not described as one, because miracles are specifically the works of Jesus, His apostles, and those given to perform miracles by gifts given only through the twelve apostles. Yet, what other word describes the magnitude of Truth's incarnation as the Son of Man, becoming a sentient, breathing, and ultimately a sacrificial man. Miraculous, beyond all natural reason; like the transformation from mans' sinful mortality to sinless immortality through obedience to His absolute Truth.

The Word as flesh becomes the Truth seen. A blind man can see it. The doubting Apostle Thomas could see it. We today can see it by faith in Christ. He exists in Truth, and Truth exists in Him; unchanging, inerrant, and certain.

Vested in Truth grows richer by the message in even simple-sounding stories from the Word, stories like the feeding of the multitude with two fish and five barley loaves, with much to spare after all had their fill. The message for me is simple, and sustaining. In darkness, when I feel all worn out and used up, Jesus is not. He always has more to give. In Him I can feast to the full, with much to spare.

Truth in the flesh of Jesus is likewise Truth in the flesh of those who follow Jesus. I must tell you about dear friends in whom I see Jesus in the flesh of their lives. They are comfortable friends; friends without pretense or varnish. These are the kind of friends you don't have to entertain; just being together and saying nothing is comfortable. They are real friends, who know your faults and still love you; who know your failures and love you more. They are laughing friends, crying friends, and sustaining friends. Now, they also have to depend more upon Jesus' supply.

The wife always gave of herself to serve others. When we were in desperate financial straits, by her doing a bag of groceries often appeared at our doorstep, though she "had nothing to do with it." She understood real love is in serving.

Now, she is learning about being used up, worn down, and worn out. She and her husband are a part of the sandwich generation – stacked between a thick slice of kids and grandkids, and a thicker slice of ailing sets of parents. Both slices are depending on her to be their filling.

Serving is her truth, and now it is a burdensome one. There's a troubled grandson who left home. Both daughters left the church, and now have unscriptural divorces. Her husband, who first survived a massive brain tumor, now has cancer. They moved from their home of forty years to care for her parents; one near blind, the other recently deceased due to Alzheimer's. She is all used up, and worn out to the point of uttering the words, "killing myself."

Those words were her cry for help, because she trusted her true friends will help. But, more than depending on friends, she'll depend upon her investment in Truth. Past her weariness and sadness, she knows the promises and provisions of God are never depleted. In Him, she can feast to the full, with much to spare. This is being vested in Truth.

Another dear couple is a testimony of faith by their investment in Truth. Their marriage is the second for each of them, following tragic, painful, and sin-laden, first marriages. His first wife was unfaithful; her first husband was sexually abusive of their daughters. Yet, each of them holds a deep conviction of the purpose, power, and promise of a committed and faithful union. Each adores the other. Their trials have not tarnished their marriage, but have gilded it.

Both of them are sustained by their investment in Truth. His, in particular, required a double investment. He had been a minister of a major denomination – one which held close to truth, but not wholly to The Truth. Following his conviction to rightly discern the Word, he understood the denomination's doctrine misses the mark. Within the conviction of God's Truth, he left the denomination to begin anew in the Lord's church.

His decision came at some painful costs. The prior ministry was monetarily a richer calling. But, he understands his calling for riches is not in the things of this world, but in the riches above. This is being vested in Truth.

A third, precious couple; both could be in a crowded room and every other person in the room would feel like their favorite child. Their family held a legacy of being vested in Truth – generations holding a shared faith in the Lord and in His church. Their riches in the Truth grew exponentially by their shared faith.

Yet, sometimes the rich blessings can be too greatly assumed. Though their lives were marked by service, it became a service with strings attached, with misguided goals. His service came with an expected return of honor. In the course of appointing elders to serve the church, he deemed the position to be his due. Pride alone disqualified him. Pride alone caused both of them to leave the church. Sadly, they forfeited their investment in Truth.

I love each of these couples. While each couple bears their sorrows, I sorrow most for the last. But, God can work even that sorrow for good, to increase my determination to be vested in Truth.

Progressing through an audit of my faith, and seeing Truth fleshed out in the lives of God's people, I have emerged from the darkness. The light is first in striving to be more like Christ, and then to become, even as an imperfect man, the flesh of Truth. Jesus calls imperfect people to accomplish His perfect plan. It is my job in whatever course He chooses, to give my life, my breath, and my voice to Truth.

Concerning lying, Richard Nixon said, "It takes two people to lie; one to tell it, and one to hear it." True enough to an extent, but it really takes three; one to tell it, one to hear it, and the third who does not refute the lie. The first two can revel in the lie if they choose, but the third person can make all the difference. The lie is sustained and spreads if no one refutes it. Certainly, in the wide realm of Christianity, there is much error taught which has not been refuted by Truth. Now, many of those lies are accepted as "a truth" or as "my truth," and are held to be just as valid because they are sincerely believed, and not refuted.

Recalling Jesus' oft-repeated phrase, "I tell you the truth," I believe He was saying more than, "Hey, guys, listen up now; you need to know this." Jesus was breathing life into the words which were the pillar and support of the apostolic mission. These are the words of which they were charged to bear witness. Their mission was to give breath and voice to these words. These are the words in which they "live and move, and have their very being" (Acts 17:28).

If I accept the call to give life, breathe, and voice to Truth, I must heed the call of the scriptures, to rightly discern the Word. I must be "ready to give an account for the hope within (me)" (I Peter 3:15), and be ready to refute the lies which burden the cause of Christ. The preparation to refute error demands continuing growth in the "nurture and admonition of the Lord" (Ephesians 6:4), and "leaving the elementary teaching about the Christ, (to) press on to maturity" (Hebrews 6:1).

My past failure of pressing on to spiritual maturity left me too weak to refute lies. In depressive periods, it left me in danger of falling away. Having so long benefited from God's grace and Truth, but not growing to a maturity which could defend His Truth, I have "put Him to an open shame." I have been like the "ground which drinks the rain which often falls on it," but I have not "brought forth vegetation useful to those for whose sake the soil is tilled." In my scriptural immaturity and in my failure to refute the lies of man, I am like the ground which "yields thorns and thistles, it is worthless and close to being cursed, and ends up being burned" (Hebrews 6:6-8).

Both Paul, in his letter to the Colossians, and Peter in his second letter, admonish "to grow in the grace and knowledge of (the) Lord." In that knowledge I can be on "guard so that (I) am not carried away by the error of unprincipled men and fall away from (my) own steadfastness" (II Peter 3:17-18).

Paul's words encourage me to "attain all the wealth that comes from the full assurance and understanding, resulting in a true knowledge of God's mystery, that is, Christ Himself." By attaining that knowledge I can be "firmly rooted and built up in Him and established in (my) faith," so that "no one takes me captive through philosophy and empty deception" (Colossians 2: 2,7-8).

In the wisdom of man, it seems so many chafe in the bridle of Truth, not wanting to submit to its direction. Perhaps, they'll wonder why I do not strain against the bridle. By my submission to Truth, some people are not surprised that I've battled persistent depression. Believing in and deferring to the absolute Truth may seem to leave no room for joy, light, and the intentions of God's grace. Some believe God would not limit the self-will and creativity of man by the bit and bridle of Truth. I feel no limitation, but instead, the certain conduit of His power. Rather than being threatened by Truth which limits self expression, I depend upon Truth as the foundation of real and balanced expression.

Truth is not the source of my darkness; it is the source of my His Light. In the crucial matters of salvation, God is proven to be truly loving and gracious by giving us inerrant and invariable Truth. I don't believe Truth is self-limiting, but is self-liberating. Through a conviction that God's wisdom is higher than my wisdom, Truth liberates me from the doubts and confusion of man's limited wisdom which is ever-changing, and unsettled.

Rather than seeing His Truth as restrictive, see it as securing. Rather than seeing it as cold and hard, black and white doctrine, see it as the foundation of spiritual confidence and assurance. Rather than Truth thwarting an expression of man's wisdom, see Truth as the cornerstone of building your life on His Most High Wisdom.

Tragically, those who disdain the concept of absolute Truth often are not rejecting Truth, but are rejecting the despicable and vicious wielding of Truth without love. When the Word is described as being sharper than a double-edged sword, some relish swinging the sword like a machete. The message of Truth is lost in the loveless messenger. Many refuse the messenger before they can accept the Truth, because Truth without love is a cold, hard burden.

As a teenager, my wife knew well her need for and the means of salvation. Though accountable to The Truth, she delayed obeying the gospel due to the cold threats of one person who repeatedly warned, "You're going to hell!" In the not-so-surprising obstinacy of a teenager, she was not going to be threatened into becoming a Christian. Certainly, that's not how God wants anyone to come. More than only to avoid hell, we come to Jesus to obtain and grow in a loving kinship with Him as we hope in Heaven.

The gospel of Christ was almost of no effect when wielded without love. Jesus' call is all about love, but His messenger forgot love is the vital conduit of Truth. If the lady had only said, "Child, I love you and want you to know the joy and assurance of His salvation," Truth would have been much earlier trusted, and much sooner obeyed. But, despite the failings of the messenger, the efficacy of Truth is through obedience. Truth alone does not save. One who knows and believes every word of Truth, relying only on knowledge, will be lost. For just as with my wife, redemption is only gained by obedience to Truth.

The Truth, the gospel unto salvation, does indeed purify us, but only if we are obedient to its demands. I Peter 1:21-23 tells us, "Since you have in *obedience* to the truth purified your souls for a sincere love of the brethren, fervently love one another from the heart." If the apostles knew every, "I tell you the truth" which Jesus spoke, but were not obedient to His Truth, Christ's mission would have faltered. Likewise, if one's investment in the Truth is only by mental ascension, the soul will never know its ascension to the heavenly home. Truth *is* the power unto salvation, but only when exercised through obedience.

In overcoming emotional darkness, the cognitive acceptance of Truth does not reveal the light. While I seldom doubted Truth, its efficacy was only realized by its application. It required the application of the Truth before the His Light could renew my spirit. Indeed, the real spiritual dividend for one's investment in Truth is realized not by knowing it, but through obeying it. In obedience to Truth we are recommended to God and eternal life. As Luke wrote in Acts 20:32, "And now I *commend* you to God and to the Word of His grace, which is able to build you up and give you the inheritance among all those who are sanctified."

Overcoming the darkness and pressing on to higher ground, I am confident in God's unchanging Truth. My dependence upon absolute Truth can be worded as in the prayer from Psalm 119.

"Forever, O Lord, Your Word is settled in Heaven. Your faith continues throughout all generations; You established the earth and it stands. They stand this day according to Your ordinances, for all things are Your servants. If Your (Truth) had not been my delight, then I would have perished in my affliction. I will never forget Your precepts, for by them You have revived me."

Yes, by His Truth He has revived me. Moving out of my darkness into His light was finally possible because I had set my focus on things above. I strove to change my focus from this life to the fixed prize of Heaven. I felt pure joy when I realized my emotional healing derives from setting my heart on the transcendent goal of Heaven. However, that proved to be a temporary understanding – there was more to learn. The point from which one sets their goal is equally crucial.

The transition from darkness to light requires two fixed points – the goal of Heaven, and a fixed foundation in the Word and the will of God. In geometric terms, the shortest path between two points is always a straight line. This assumes the two points remain fixed. Starting from point "A" and drawing a straight line towards point "B" requires both points to remain constant. If "B" moves, the line becomes much longer, but if "A" moves after starting to draw the line there is no connection made. Connecting the dots of my life, point "A" is the constant, fixed, inerrant Truth of God's Word. Point "B" is the victory of my heavenly home. Not until I identified the points could I make the connection to His light.

The understanding of His words continues to unfold. Now I cherish Psalm 119. Each of the stanzas of this psalm reinforces the need for a sure foundation in the Truth as we pursue His will and focus on the ultimate victory of Heaven.

The stanza, Nun, scripturally draws the straight line which connects the starting point in Truth, and the ending point in Heaven. It speaks of one who is striving to move from mental anguish into the light.

"Your word is a lamp to my feet and a light to my path. I have sworn and I will confirm it, that I will keep Your ordinances. I am exceedingly afflicted; revive me, O Lord, according to Your word. O, accept the freewill offerings of my mouth, O Lord, and teach me your ordinances. My life is continually in my hand, yet I do not forget Your law. The wicked have laid a snare for me, yet I have not gone astray from Your precepts. I have inherited Your testimonies forever, for they are the joy of my heart. I have inclined my heart to perform Your statutes forever, even to the end."

We may chafe within the constraints of Truth, the course set along a narrow way to pass through a narrow gate. Whether concerning our salvation, or His direction for our lives, it is within the temptations of man to seek a broader way. Can we understand the benefits of His Truth as being like the forces of a mighty river? A river flowing wide and shallow across the plains obscures its real power beneath its quiet, slowly drifting surface. Yet, when the river is constrained in a deep and narrow gorge, its sound intensifies like the roaring thunder and its true, awesome power is revealed.

In our spiritual river, flowing broadly and meandering by our self-will, what little power is ours? His Word meandering through the broader ways of man's wisdom bears little effect. But, in submission to His will, true power is revealed through us as living waters forced through the narrow gate. As for me, I've followed my broad and powerless course. My truth – a hybrid of Truth, my experiences, and past imbalanced thinking – could never bring real contentment or a real hope of Heaven. I'll now choose His narrow course, His Truth, and be glad in it.

Why do we wrestle, viewing Truth as constrictive, rather than constructive? Why do we see truth as bearing a millstone which limits our lives, rather than as the tried and true cornerstone on which to build our lives? Those conflicting perceptions of Truth relate to our perceptions of what it means to be a child of the King.

We are told "unless you become as a child, you will not enter the kingdom of Heaven. He says, "Permit the little children to come to me; do not hinder them; for the kingdom of God belongs to such as these" (Luke 18:16). The call is not to be childish, but to be child-like; not to be careless, but to be careful, trustful, and heedful of His direction.

Do we ever forget our own fearful, timid yet trusting steps in the middle of the night as we sought refuge and security, snug in our parents' bed? If we have forgotten, we are reminded by our children or grandchildren pressing for refuge at our side in the darkness. What sweeter comfort, what sweeter bond is there between a parent and child? And, what sweeter submission is there than to come before God in simple, childlike faith, pressing for refuge at His side, to know the comfort of His certain Truth?

Like a fearful child, do we ever get over our fear of the dark? Our fiercest foes, whether imagined in extreme thoughts, or real in the tragedies of this life, are worse in our darkness. While in the fullness of day we seek our own ways, in our darkness we seek the refuge of His ways. This refuge is the call to live in the Light, as He is in the Light. Thriving in His secure and sustaining light is only accomplished by our investment and submission to His Truth.

The power of Truth is not simply the knowledge of it. The real power is by the telling of Truth. But, if one is not vested in Truth, there is a strong temptation to compromise the message. Certainly, for anyone like me who has fought a fear of conflict and confrontation, the Dark Angel tempts us to hedge the Word. We must remember that contending for Truth is not going nose to nose, battling over minutia which changes nothing, but is upholding the Truth which is the Power to change everything.

As a voice for Truth, I must remember there can be no compromising of the essential Gospel. The inherent nature of compromise demands moving away from Truth. If one's position represents Truth and life, and another's position represents error and death, any compromise to a point in the middle removes us from Truth. Akin to knowing faith without works is dead, faith based upon compromised truth is, at the least, critically wounded.

Similarly, as we are warned to be either hot or cold, the Truth is never cold, but is like a fire. Indeed, our God Himself "is a consuming fire" (Hebrews 12:29). "My Word is Truth, declares the Lord. Is not my Word like fire" (Jeremiah 24:28-29)? Remember, just as fire does not flame from cold coals, faith does not flame from tepid truth.

Recalling the many dangers and hardships Paul faced, it takes far less dangers for many to revoke their investment in the Truth. Yet, Paul's faith would not be shaken. Perhaps, he held the same mindset as Job, who felt God's hand heavy upon him, but knew, "When He has tested me I shall come forth as gold." Job was vested in Truth, saying, "My foot has held fast to His path; I have kept to His way and not turned aside. I have not departed from the command of His lips" (Job 23:12).

The desire to be vested in Truth is tandem with continually looking for that city. The desire for an unshakable faith is also for an unshakable inheritance in that city, His unshakable kingdom. Remember the warning in Hebrews 13:

"See to it that you don't refuse Him who is speaking. For if those did not escape when they refused Him who warned them on earth, much less will we escape who turn away from Him who warns from Heaven. And His voice shook the earth then, but now He has promised saying, 'Yet once more I will shake not only the earth, but also the Heaven.' This expression, 'Yet once more,' denotes the removing of those things which can be shaken, as of created things, so that those things which cannot be shaken may remain. Therefore, since we receive a kingdom which cannot be shaken, let us show gratitude, by which we may offer to God an acceptable service with reverence and awe."

Acceptable service must be grounded upon my investment in the unshakable Truth of God. I, for far too long, invested in my truth which could be shaken. My truth was informed more by my past than by His Word. My truth failed. But, His Truth prevails, and I will prevail in His Truth as I continue looking for that city.

SEVEN

WHAT MUST I DO?

In the mountains near my home in Idaho, it is spellbinding to watch as a climber ascending a sheer cliff assesses every grip and toehold. Every meticulous placement is tested; every position is anchored for the next. From each hold he surveys every crevice and niche, planning the surest way to the next ledge, and to the summit. Recalling the verse which exhorts, "work out your salvation with fear and trembling," like a mountaineer, I must be certain of every scriptural footing, testing every anchor's hold.

Seeking higher ground, I must first be standing on solid ground, and anchored in the cleft of the Solid Rock. Seeking to climb above the darkness, I must be sure I'm not climbing alone. For the mountain climber, or for those seeking to overcome mental illness, every grip and toehold must seek, "What must I do?"

While pursuing a second-half-of-life career change, I built friendships which challenged my thinking on many levels. These friends are culturally, philosophically and religiously far more liberal than me. The compass points of our views are as opposite as east is from west, but hearing their views challenges me to confirm my beliefs as the certain foundation for my life. The grips and toeholds of one's beliefs, if valid for reaching the summit, should withstand the testing of conflicting views.

How did views counter to mine affect my faith? When confronted with radically opposing views on either social or religious issues, was I shocked because I felt the norms of my life were threatened? Or, was I troubled because the other position violates the will of God? If I am shocked because opposing views threatens my values, I am only a cultural Christian; that is, Christian only in my lifestyle and habits. A cultural Christian reduces faith to a set of issues serving his own causes, whether or not his causes serve the higher cause of Christ. A true Christian is one who takes a stand, not to affirm his own will, but to affirm the will of God.

I must know which I am – a cultural Christian, or a true Christian, intently drawing closer to the will of God. It amounts to whether the name "Christian" is an adjective or a noun. Is the name only part of a description of me, or is it my identity? Is "Christian" truly who I am?

I, and any Christian still living in persistent darkness, must be willing to ask why? Why am I not enjoying a measure of His peace and contentment? Am I suffering because I demand more than God demands to be reconciled to Him? Have I depended too much on self and too little upon Jesus? Somewhere within the answers are the clues of my darkness.

The mindset I've used for those answers is from the words of the second verse of *Higher Ground:*

My heart has no desire to stay
Where doubts arise and fears dismay;
Tho' some may dwell where these abound,
My prayer, my aim is higher ground.

The prodigal son could not know the blessings of being reunited with his father, without first being reconciled with him. In the same manner, I must be reconciled with God to know the blessings of kinship with Him. The sum of all scripture is for the reconciliation of mankind unto God, towards an intimate and fruitful kinship; ultimately, to an eternal union with Him in Heaven.

How am I set upon solid ground with God and into the confident assurance of a heavenly home? Beyond my own need, has any single question so driven the thinking of man, and so divided the purposes and fortunes of man?

Not an anomaly of our present age, this tendency to divide has always been. In learning about the New Covenant, the great challenge before the Israelites was separating their old traditions and learning from the better way of the Savior. From the start there arose such divisions that Paul, in his first letter to the church in Corinth, exhorted them for unity in the new way of Christ. Already there were quarrels among them based upon by whom they were baptized. As Paul wrote, "... each of you is saying, 'I am of Paul', and 'I am of Apollos', and 'I am of Cephas', and 'I am of Christ.' "

Fast forwarding through the centuries, the divisions persist. People strive for salvation based upon man's reasoning. To this present generation, the Apostle Paul's letter would read, "I am of Joel Osteen, I am of Max Lucado, and I am of Pope Benedict." Following with the same question Paul asked of the Corinthians, "Has Christ been divided?"

In purposing to step out as a soldier of the cross by following His commands, I must know I am in his army. Since, Jesus is "the way, the truth, and [the means unto] life" I must be in step with Christ. Seeking to be in step, the divisive issue still is baptism. By which baptism, if any, and at what point relative to baptism am I reconciled to God, and added to His army?

I have an unusual heritage of having been baptized for every reason by which men cling to a purpose in water baptism. The first two baptisms were at early ages. First, I was born into a religious tradition which practices a baptism by the sprinkling of infants, as a consecration of my life to the Lord until I attained an age of confirming my faith. But, most of my growing up years was within a different religious belief. I was baptized by immersion as an outward testimony of a previous inward experience. This followed asking Jesus to save me, with the understanding that I was saved prior to baptism. Therefore, the baptism was an affirmation of the salvation, and an affiliation with the denomination.

Lastly, as an adult, I was baptized by immersion for the forgiveness of my sins, and to receive the indwelling of the Holy Spirit. This baptism was according to my conviction that the baptism itself was necessary unto salvation, and my salvation was imputed in baptism.

Which baptism is correct? All three derive from varied interpretations of the scriptures. Which is God's plan? Many seem to throw up their hands in confusion and propose that by God's grace all beliefs are right simply because all have in some form called upon the name of the Lord. But, "God is not a God of confusion" (I Corinthians 14:33). Man who creates the confusion. Compounding the problem, many argue it's a matter of each one's interpretation. Many will miss Christ's call unto redemption simply because of the confusion created by mans' divisions.

Beyond which baptism is the "one baptism" which leads to salvation; what is a Christian? By societies' standards, a Christian subscribes to a set of values, living a good life according to a set of biblical ethics. Or, in the political arena, you're a Christian by voting according to a prescribed set of political issues. Voting for the candidate who claims some standing on a Christian-values platform defines one as a Christian. Simpler still, by claiming a belief in God to some degree, or by simply being a good person, in the world's confusion, makes one a Christian.

Which definition glorifies God and leads to reconciliation to God through Christ? Some make tradition their gospel; some make sincerity to a preferred interpretation their doctrine. Some endeavor to rightly discern God's will through the Word. And, though the scripture says, rhetorically, "even the foolishness of God is higher than the wisdom of man" (I Corinthians 1:25), many teach a purely humanistic doctrine; sprinkling in a few scriptural references just to give the color and hollow ringing of truth.

Should I just accept, "Oh, just believe, it will all work out because God is love?" It seems for the vain appearance of unity in, many have adopted the mindset of, "Can't we all just get along? Let's agree to peaceably disagree and trust Jesus' grace to cover the difference."

While salvation is possible *only* through faith in God's grace, that grace does not change the very nature of God. Unlike the whims of mankind, our heavenly Father's will does not change; He is the same yesterday, today and tomorrow. In Him "there is no variation or shifting shadow" (James 1:17). While the will of mankind throughout the centuries has often changed concerning what is needful unto salvation, the Word assures me, God does not in any way change. His will is exercised in His unchanging nature as loving and merciful; but also as just and jealous.

By His unchanging nature, I must adhere to His Word and His will, within the covenant of grace, just as others formerly did under the Law. From Eden to Zion, God's nature is the same. His New Covenant of grace only changes two matters - the means of reconciliation and the means of worship.

As unchanging as the very nature of God, so too, is the Word itself. Beyond any variable standard of man, the Word is the only certain standard. Without a conviction and a submission to the authority of the Word as absolute Truth, and the only means to know and to be known of God, all other doctrine is moot.

Salvation ultimately requires my submission, as from the heart of a child. A friend recently shared with her young grandson the story of Absalom; the story so full of sin, conspiracy, deception and death. Afterward, the child asked if she thought Absalom went to Heaven when he died. Trying to assure him of God's loving nature, seeking to put a positive spin to the tragic story, she allowed that if Absolom ask for forgiveness, then perhaps so.

Wise beyond his years, her grandson said, "Nana, it doesn't say that in the Bible, and you can't change it." Oh my, out of the mouths of babes comes truth. We should all know it so simply, "You can't change it."

What then is needful for salvation? And, how can I, or anyone, though "saved," know without a doubt my standing with Him? In the simplest of terms, reconciliation requires three things – a soul seeking, the Word teaching, and Jesus redeeming. That is all!

It does not matter what I say, for no one is accountable to my beliefs, but rather to God's Word. It does not matter what Osteen, Lucado, or Benedict say. One preacher correctly has said pertaining to his judgment of others' teachings about salvation, "I am not called to say who will be condemned. I am called to tell people how to be saved." As Jesus said, "God did not send His Son into the world to condemn the world, but to save the world through Him" (John 3:17).

While I am accountable to a covenant of grace, do I have liberty to choose my ways of belief, of worship, and of salvation? I am to "work out [my] salvation with all fear and trembling" before an all-powerful and jealous God. But, working out my own salvation does not permit salvation on my own terms. Because Jesus is the only way, I come to the Father only by His terms.

II Peter 1:20-21, is worth remembering in any issue which divides us. "But know this first of all, that no prophecy of Scripture is a matter of one's own interpretation, for no prophecy was ever made by an act of human will, but men moved by the Holy Spirit spoke from God." The scriptures were preexistent with God, for "in the beginning was the Word, and the Word was with God, and the Word was God" (John 1:1).

Many scriptures speak to the requirement of water baptism for salvation, often mentioning baptism and salvation within the same verse. Note the pattern, baptism always precedes salvation. In all matters, the Word speaks full well, alone, without any interpretation of man. To that end, consider only God's Word.

"For he who has believed and has been baptized shall be saved; but he who has disbelieved shall be condemned" (Mark 16:16).

"Repent and each one of you be baptized in the name of Jesus Christ for the forgiveness of your sins; and you will receive the gift of the Holy Spirit" (Acts 2:38).

"Or do you not know that all of us who have been baptized into Christ Jesus have been baptized into His death? Therefore we have been buried with Him through baptism into death, so that as Christ was raised from the dead through the glory of the father, so we too might walk in newness of life" (Romans 6: 3-4).

"Now why do you delay? Get up and be baptized, and wash away your sins, calling on His name" (Acts 22:16).

I will, however, comment on one scripture solely because it is so widely known out of its context, leading to misunderstanding. "For God so loved the world that He gave His only begotten Son, that whosoever believes in Him shall not perish, but have eternal life." If there is any scripture the world can identify by its book, chapter, and verse, it is John 3:16. We see it on bumper stickers, and hanging on railings at football games. It perhaps qualifies as America's favorite verse which, for it is held up as the sum of all which is needed for salvation. It is a summation of the gospel, but it is not all which is needful for reconciliation with God.

To apply the verse properly to salvation, it must be placed back into its context. It is only one verse from a conversation between Jesus and Nicodemus concerning the new birth. It follows Jesus' words, "I tell you the truth, no one can see the kingdom of God, unless he is born again" (John 3:3-4).

To use John 3:16 alone misses the full meaning. Jesus spoke those words as a restating of an entire conversation, just as we reiterate a point at the conclusion of a discussion. Holding to only one verse for what is needful unto salvation, it should be the verse which amplifies John 3:16; which is John 3:5. "I tell you the truth; no one can enter the kingdom of God unless he is born of water and the Spirit." The "born again," of verse 16, is the "born of water and the Spirit," in verse 5.

I trust the Lord's grace, but I dare not to stand before the Righteous Judge without following the entire plan of salvation, including immersion for the remission of my sins. To do any less depends only on my wisdom, and negates the purpose of depending on God for renewal.

Seeking the assurance of my salvation reveals the continuing need for repentance as I seek to overcome my darkness and spiritual mediocrity. "For the *sorrow* that is according to the will of God produces a repentance without regret, leading to salvation, but the sorrow of the world produces death" (II Corinthians 7:10). I'm convinced the *sorrow* which is according to the will of God also works in my transformation from darkness into the light, for it is repentance without regret.

My salvation is not merited through my decision to be immersed in water, for *nothing* I can do merits salvation. Neither is it *solely* by the water, for water *alone* does not save; however, "baptism now saves you" (I Peter 3:21). By baptism, alike in pattern to Jesus' death, burial, and resurrection, salvation is received through the grace of God. I am persuaded, baptism is essential to my salvation. Therefore, as I strive to find higher ground, ever looking for that city, I do so convinced of my standing on Christ's solid ground through salvation according to Truth of His Word.

Many people take exception with the assertion there is only one way to salvation, and that baptism is necessary. For any struggling to move from darkness into the light, may the struggle spur a willingness to take one more look. By studying the Word one more time, we will confirm our understanding of the Word, and thereby gain a greater assurance of our faith; or we'll find God's Truth plainly, without the varnish of man's words. We are winners either way, simply by taking one more look.

Other people may regard me as being brainwashed. I'm not offended by the pejorative intent of the label. For, within the will of God, isn't this the purpose of His Son? Indeed, my mind, heart, and soul all need His washing. The washing does not render me mindless to do my will; it makes me mindful to do God's will.

Others may regard me as a legalist, much as the Pharisees who sought to bind Christians to parts of the old law. I earnestly pray I, or none like me, am like the wretched Pharisees. They were admonished,

> "But woe to you, scribes and Pharisees, hypocrites, because you shut off the kingdom of Heaven from people; for you do not enter in yourselves, nor do you allow those who are entering to go in" (Matthew 23:13).

Certainly, there is no gain in binding upon myself a false teaching of baptism, for in doing so I lose all hope of entering the kingdom of God. But, I hold to this understanding because the scriptures also teach me to,

> "Enter through the narrow gate; for the gate is wide and broad is the way that leads to destruction, and there are many who enter it. For the way is small and the way is narrow that leads to life, and

there are few who find it" (Matthew 7: 13-14).

I did not set the distance between the gateposts. Jesus did; and He, Himself, calls the distance narrow. Those who set the posts much wider, do so from their understanding of grace, desiring to see all brought to the Father through Jesus. But, they are seeking to bring the lost to Christ's salvation through a standard to which God will say, 'I never knew you; depart from me" (Matthew 7: 23).

How narrow are the gateposts set? We can't walk through still clinging to another master (Matthew 6:24). We can't walk through clinging to our treasures (Matthew 6:21). We can't enter still clinging to another standard (Col 2:8-23). We can't enter while dragging a load of deeds done in one's own name (Matthew 23:5). And, we cannot enter by salvation in any other name than Christ (Acts 4:12). The gateposts are set just wide enough for a soul clothed in the spotless robe of Jesus to pass through.

My friend, Virgil, tells about his experience in the Coast Guard, following the narrow way, versus the broad way. From Miami, he charted a course towards port in St. John's, Newfoundland. It seems fairly obvious to aim northward along the coast toward the harbor. Yet, he learned aiming but not staying truly on course, varying by only one degree, will cast the ship hundreds of miles away from the intended harbor. The harbor into Heaven is narrow. The course is well charted by the Word of God, with Jesus piloting the way.

There is no fault in the Word of God as I seek salvation. God's Word is all I need to obey. With certainty, I can know what is needful to be known by God. In seeking higher ground, moving beyond spiritual or emotional darkness, I can confidently live on a plane above "where doubts arise and fears dismay."

Hand in hand with the knowledge of salvation, there persists another doubt and division among those seeking God. Once redeemed, do we live in an irrevocable trust of salvation; a salvation which cannot be lost? Or, can we forfeit our salvation and our vested inheritance in Heaven?

It seems inherent with the mindset of our culture to check off the "To Do" lists in our lives. We want to complete a task and feel like, "Well, I'm all done with that – good to go now!" It's much like I remember about Sunday school as a child. We had weekly offering envelopes on which was a row of boxes to check for each thing done for class. One box was for, "Brought Bible," another read, "Studied Lesson." And, there were boxes for "On Time," "Gave Offering," "Invited Someone," and several more. If you checked all the boxes, your grade was "100". We'd like all spiritual issues to be so straight-forward – check off the boxes, and be done with it. But, we are called to keep on keeping on; steadfast to the end.

Can I lose my salvation? My experience includes a time of belief in both sides of the question – either "eternal security," or "condition-al grace." I was raised in a religious tradition which teaches once a person is saved, nothing can separate one from salvation; in essence, "once saved; always saved." No matter the course of life following salvation, many people trust all sin is covered by grace, and their home in Heaven is assured. They rightly believe nothing can separate us from the love of God, which is true. But, can anything separate us from our salvation?

In the heartfelt need to know the certainty of my salvation, why wouldn't God want me to soar along without Him? His Word paints a picture of me being lifted up to soar like an eagle. Yes, but I am not an eagle – it is God who lifts me up to soar. As with the Jews deliver-ance from Pharaoh's army, God said, "you have seen what I did to the Egyptians and how I bore you on eagles' wings and brought you to myself" (Exodus 19:4). I must depend upon Him, for only through Him, as He lifts me up, can I spiritually soar like an eagle, landing safely on eternity's shore.

I believe now the view counter to "eternal security." I hold the conviction I can lose my salvation; not negating God's grace, but believing that by returning to *willful, persistent* sinning I choose to remove myself from the covering of grace. Just as in the matters of baptism, I can know which view – eternal security or conditional grace, is of God.

In the infinite love of God, and the matchless grace of Jesus, can anything separate me from my salvation and the hope of Heaven? The Bible assures me of my victory in Christ. The Apostle Paul wrote,

"Who will separate us from the love of Christ? Will tribulation, or distress, or persecution, or famine, or nakedness, or peril, or sword? For your sake we are being put to death all day long, we were considered as sheep to be slaughtered. But in all things we overwhelmingly conquer through Him who loved us. For I am convinced that neither death, nor life, nor angels, nor principalities, nor things present, nor things to come, nor powers, nor height, nor depth, nor any created thing, will be able to separate us from the love of God, which is in Christ Jesus our Lord" (Romans 8:39).

Romans 8, is a precious assurance of my victory through Christ. Certainly, it is the highest desire of God's heart that I come to know Him through the redemption in Jesus Christ. How could a loving God withdraw His grace, His mercy, or the promise of salvation? God does not withdraw His promises, for it is man who withdraws from God by *willful, persistent* sin.

Again, the answer derives from God's unchanging nature, for God's will does not change according to the shifting wisdom and whims of man" (James 1:17). He is forever the same. Only His covenant of redemption changed; His character did not. While I revel in God's love, provision, and promise, I must remember He is a jealous God, meaning He is passionate about His will. He will not be mocked, either by the people of the Old Covenant, or by me, as one redeemed of the New Covenant. In the very simplest of terms, God is God, sin is sin, and *willful, persistent* sin which mocks His plan of redemption, separates me from our salvation.

Romans 8, in promising nothing can separate me from the love of God, is speaking only of the tools of the Dark Angel. Tribulations, persecution, and the sword are from the enemy. The enemy cannot separate me from the love of God. The passage, however, does not mention sin, which will separate me from my salvation. Sin is the only thing which God will not forbear. God will not be in the presence of sin. My willful sins "crucify the Son again, holding Him to an open shame," which mocks God's plan of redemption (Hebrews 6:6).

It is not God's desire for me to be separated, for He created me to bring glory to Him. However, every sin must be avenged. If I *persist* outside of reconciliation and outside of Jesus' continuing redemption, my sin has not been avenged. God has often sought a reason not to exercise His wrath upon those who willfully persist in sin. At times, God relented, but God is still "the avenger of their evil deeds" (Psalm 99:8). And, while God is willing through Christ to forgive me again and again, I know there is a day of judgment when God will have grown tired of my willful sinning. He will avenge; judgment must come! In that day, if I have removed myself from the covering of His grace, He will declare to me, the words He spoke to Israel. "You have forsaken Me. You keep going backward so I will stretch out My hand against You and destroy you; I am tired of relenting" (Jeremiah 15:6).

It is not God's desire to be separated from me, for separation negates the purpose of the Perfect Sacrifice. Yet, if I *willfully persist* in sin, I lose God's favor. "There remains no sacrifice" (Hebrews 10:26), for Christ's blood does not cover the unrepentant.

The writer of Hebrews admonished those who knew the Truth and had left the former way. But, they were uncertain, still needing to learn again the simple things. In their spiritual immaturity, they were warned against falling away.

"For in the case of those who have once been enlightened and have tasted the heavenly gift and have been made partakers of the Holy Spirit, and have tasted the good word of God and the powers of the age to come, and then have fallen away, it is impossible to renew them again to repentance, since they again crucify to themselves the Son of God and put Him to an open shame."

The writer encouraged them in their diligence, saying, show "diligence to the *very end*, in order to make your hope sure" (Hebrews 6:9). The promise of God is real and sure, yet requires our diligence in seeking the way of Christ unto the very end.

In context, Philippians 2, the exhortation to "work out your salvation with fear and trembling," is speaking to those who have already been saved. Paul is encouraging them to continue in the faith, saying, "So then, my beloved, just as you have always obeyed…work out your salvation with fear and trembling." Certainly I'm not saved by my works, for "it is God who is at work in (me), both to will and to work for His good pleasure" (Philippians 2:13). It requires me to continue to obey.

Peter wrote in his second letter, exhorting Christians to grow in their faith and knowledge of Christ. Peter reinforces Paul's teaching, encouraging people to "look forward to a new Heaven and a new earth, the home of the righteous" (II Peter 3:13). Peter warns, against those who distort scriptural truths, saying, "Beware lest you also fall from your own steadfastness, being led away with the error of the wicked." Further, Peter warns those who by their own sinful desires distort the Truth. To them, and to any who are drawn away with them, he writes,

"For if, after they have escaped the defilements of the world by the knowledge of the Lord and Savior Jesus Christ, they are again entangled with them and overcome, by this he is enslaved. For it would be better for them not to have known the way of righteousness, than having known it, to turn away from the holy commandment handed to them."

Painting the picture in plain words, Peter adds, "It has happened to them according to the true proverb, 'A dog returns to its own vomit,' and, 'a sow, after washing, returns to wallow in the mire'" (II Peter 2:20-22). Thus, from Peter's words, we must know God will not be mocked by our turning away from Him.

One of the clearest refutations of the teaching of eternal security, or "once saved; always saved", is in the book of Hebrews. Again, the teaching is a call to grow in confident faith and to persevere to the end.

"Let us hold fast the confession of our hope without wavering, for He who promised is faithful. For if we go on sinning willfully after receiving the knowledge of truth, there no longer remains a sacrifice for our sins, but a terrifying expectation of judgment and the fury of a fire which will consume the adversaries."

Truly, if there no longer remains a sacrifice, there no longer remains salvation. One's choice to "go on sinning willfully," becoming "once again entangled in them," is the basis for conditional grace.

Even more than the punishment of earth due to those who sinned against the Old Covenant, the scripture asks, "How much severer punishment do you think he will deserve who has trampled under foot the Son of God, and has regarded as unclean the blood of the covenant by which he was sanctified." Then comes the warning; "It is a terrifying thing to fall into the hands of the living God." Finally, I am encouraged, "For you have need of endurance, so that when you have done the will of God, (inferring the need for future action) you may receive what was promised" (Hebrews 10:23, 26-27, 29, 31, and 36).

While confidently looking for that city, this is what I seek. In a message to the church in Sardis, by Jesus' own words,

"You have a few people in Sardis who have not soiled their garments; they will walk with me in white, for they are worthy. He who overcomes will thus be clothed in white garments; and I will not erase his name from the book of life, and I will confess his name before My Father and before the angels" (Revelation 3:4-5).

Revelations 3 tells us what can sever the relationship – my *persistent, willful* sin. Jesus assures to those who overcome by continuing to walk in His Way, their name will never be erased from the Book of Life. Trusting that promise requires the opposite to also be true. The names of those who do not walk in His way will be erased from the Book. I hold to my salvation by holding to Hebrews 3:14. "We have become partakers of Christ *if* we hold the beginning of our confidence steadfast to the end." "If" is the basis of conditional grace.

The truths concerning grace are unquestionable. His grace is infinite, it is freely given, and it is unmerited. We tend to add those truths together and reach the sum of eternal security. But, even Jesus' words make it conditional. "I am the way, the truth, and the life, no man comes to the Father *except* through me. "Except" is the basis of conditional grace.

Paul, in his letter to the Galatians, confronted their unfaithfulness to the Truth they had known. "Now that you know God – or rather or known by God – how is it that you are turning back to those weak and miserable principles? Do you wish to be enslaved again?" Previously, they had received him warmly, caring for him in his time of need. Yet, after confronting them, Paul, suffering from their scorn asks, "Have I now become your enemy for telling you the truth?"

That same question now speaks to my fear. Have I, too, now become your enemy? For a person who grew up trying to make no waves, have I now done just that?

As I look forward to that city, in all of its radiant splendor and ceaseless joy, I must remember the command to help others find His way. Oh, how sad it will be to face the judgment, in the earnest expectation of Heavenly, but then to hear, as from a beggar, "You never mentioned Him to me." Is there a stronger motivation for marching onward in the calling of the Lord?

Still, my primary desire for studying what is needful for salvation is to establish my confidence in my standing with God. I have included my search for a steadfast assurance of my salvation, not as a source of conflict, but as a statement of the bedrock importance of a confident kinship with Christ. The cornerstone of anyone's search for light must be the in their relationship with God, for ultimately all will give an answer to the Truth.

Since I've taken one more look, I am confident of many things – foremost is a greater assurance of my salvation and my hope in Heaven. By taking one more look, I am more confident in the Spirit's working in all things for good. I am also convinced God worked through those new friendships, not to prove them wrong or to prove myself right, but to establish my faith as the foundation of healing, and of my hope in Heaven with Him.

So, what must I do? I'll follow the answer given to those who asked at Pentecost, "Brethren, what shall we do? Peter said to them, "Repent, and each one of you be baptized in the name of Jesus Christ for the forgiveness of your sins" (Acts 2:37-38). And, what else must I do? I will remember Jesus' own words, "…he who endures to the end will be saved" (Mark 13:13).

I am convinced those who are yearning to overcome their own emotional darkness must truly know who they are in relation to God. They must trust fully the beliefs on which they base their hopes for peace and light. Whatever structure of mind one builds atop that foundation, it cannot endure the storms without being set on the knowledge of their true identity. When our lives are tested in the crucible, will our core beliefs stand up to the heat? If not, we'll never find our way to the true Light, Jesus.

For those like me who have struggled too long in darkness, trust God to work through your sufferings. Do not lose heart. From within the fiery crucible of your innermost darkness, God's greatest blessings are revealed. From the darkest trials your highest dreams are born in the full light of Jesus' leading; even the highest dream of Heaven

EIGHT

MIGHTY OR REAL?

"If anyone thinks himself to be religious, and yet does not bridle his tongue, but deceives his own heart, this man's religion is worthless" (James 1:26). These words indicted and convicted me for the duplicity of my spiritual life.

I had presumed overcoming darkness was only a battle of leaving my past and negative thinking behind; just "forgetting what is behind and pressing on to what is ahead." I soon confronted another battle – overcoming the words of my mouth. I confronted the condemning reality, "the things that proceed out of the mouth come from the heart, and defile the man" (Matthew 15:18). The words of my heart revealed a defiled and double-minded man.

I had known it for a long time, but in a pattern of living darkly, I accepted my defiled words as my justifiable venting of frustration and anger. The evidences of being a defiled and double-minded man grew from an invitation to speak for a men's retreat which focused on becoming a "mighty man" of God. Specifically, I addressed how I am a mighty man of God while at work. I could think of several men I considered mighty in their walk with the Lord. But, when I compared a mental picture of them with a picture of myself at work, I looked nothing like them.

Being a mighty man of God at work brings to mind an old Firestone tire commercial from the Sixties. The camera shot of a car traveling down the highway, zoomed in close to the front tire rolling on the pavement. The ad's jingle sang, "Wherever wheels are rolling, no matter what the load; the name to know is Firestone, where the rubber meets the road."

If Christianity is a road trip, being a Christian on the job is the defining, "rubber meets the road" issue. As men, no matter what the loads of our lives, the job is where we prove our character. There's not much challenge in being a man of God within the church walls, but being a Christian on the job can be quite a bumpy road, indeed. I had to admit my Christianity wasn't getting much traction. Spiritually, my tires weren't tracking true. I needed realignment and rebalancing. I was sliding off the road, having lost my grip by the slippery words of my mouth.

Perhaps, I worked among a unique set of people. They were my rationalization for living double-mindedly. My employer claimed to be God; not just as the boss, but he meant it with a capital "G". He seriously told me, "I do not sin." I worked with several men whose religion teaches they will become a god. Most others believed they have no need of God. Several had great fun following the advice of a psychic. And, the real show-stopper was a homosexual who saw nothing amiss about dressing up for Halloween as Jesus Christ, complete with a crown of thorns.

Essentially, every one of them, even the religious ones among them had one thing in common – they were living according to their own self-righteous standards. So, the challenge there was to live according to a different standard; to not be self-righteous, but to depend upon Jesus' righteousness.

However, by assessing them as being self-righteous, I often fell into another self-righteous trap. By the thinking errors, I thought, "God, I thank you that I am not like other people..." (Matthew 18:11). Yes, I became like the Pharisee who counted himself as righteous, and viewed others with contempt. I had to admit I am by my own unrighteousness no better than anyone.

In some ways, I did pretty well at as a man of God, particularly in honesty concerning financial matters. Among the companies where I've worked, I was expected to suborn many financial improprieties, including felony fraud. But, my employers came to know I'd have no part in it. In matters involving money, they knew I'd bring the relevant information, but leave the freewheeling dealing to them. Or, in dealing with customers, when one employer said, "Oh, I'll take care of this one," it meant he was up to some shenanigans, and he knew I wouldn't handle it his way.

People knew I wouldn't drink at company get-togethers, or if they were scheduled on Wednesday nights, I'd be at church. The guys in the warehouse knew it was me who left the radio tuned to Christian stations. But, by those small measures, thinking of me as more righteous was utter foolishness. Even the notion of being "more righteous" was foolishness – there are no degrees of righteousness. One is righteous only because it is imputed by God in an obedient response to faith. Besides, all too often, the good I have done as a man of God hasn't mattered a bit. The good was negated by the surest witness against my credibility as a Christian – my careless tongue.

As I began to strive for a spiritually higher plane, I became increasingly troubled by the words of my mouth. They were never lying words and seldom were cursing words, yet they could be vile and vicious. Increasingly, I began to understand James' words; while thinking myself to be religious I was deceived by my unbridled tongue. My religion and my example as a man of God were worthless. No matter the show of religion I offered, it was defiled by my tongue, revealing my duplicitous, angry heart.

I recall from years ago a minister preaching against the tendency of many in the church to speak coarsely, or tell a crude joke. Beyond the obvious admonition against cursing, he knew the coarse jokes revealed spiritual weakness and corrupted our witness.

His warning certainly applied to me, but speaking coarsely was an easy trap to slip into at work. In managing men mostly of younger ages, mostly of different religious and moral values, it was difficult to make any connection with them. In wanting to be more than the guy who told them what to do, conversation often flowed to the lowest common denominator of values. In the typical nature of men to avoid discussing matters of real worth, crude conversation prevailed. And, the desire for a measure of camaraderie prevailed over my intentions to be a man of God.

This rationale sufficed for a while, but it was a lie. Camaraderie with employees was not the culprit; the stores of my heart were. "The good man brings good things out of the good stored up in his heart, and the evil man brings evil things out of the evil stored up in his heart. For out of the overflow of his heart his mouth speaks" (Luke 6:45).

"Overflow" is the condemning word for the evil-hearted man, or for the double-minded man. As either, we delude ourselves into believing our duplicity will not be seen. We speak righteously among the righteous, unless their tongue is also wagging evilly, and we speak carelessly among those who are careless. Many who claim to be righteous prove themselves to be careless about righteousness. We think we can hide the evil thoughts, but when among the careless, the evil words flow.

This, too, sounds like a rationalization, much like the Sixties-era comic, Flip Wilson's alter ego, Geraldine, "The devil made me do it;" meaning we only spoke carelessly because others did. Perhaps so, but the Dark Angel can't reveal evil thoughts if the heart does not hold them to overflowing. Therefore, the striving for higher ground demands replacing all which is evil with all which is holy until the heart overflows with the good.

It is a reminder of mans' finite power which makes one admit he cannot trick the tongue to hide the stores of his heart. The tongue will not be coerced to speak pure words when the stores of the heart are mostly of sour words. When I spoke in ways I should not, it was insufficient to simply will myself to speak as I ought. Situations often arose in which the stores of my heart were revealed. Those moments proved the words of Paul, "For what I want to do, I do not do, but what I hate, I do" (Romans 7:15).

As soon as my tongue revealed my heart, I was ashamed. Thankfully, this measure of shame was evidence the Spirit had not given up on me. God was intent on working His good will in me.

The tongue draws from the well of words deep within our hearts. If the water in the well is pure, the words will be sweet. If the water is sour, so will be the words. No amount of willing the water to taste sweet can change the taste. The soured water must be replaced by the sweetest water from the Purest Stream. Not until I purposed to store pure waters in my heart, allowing the Spirit's filtering of the water through the Word, could I begin to change the words of my mouth.

A challenge to becoming a mighty man of God is in confusing the business world's concept of mighty with God's precepts for being mighty. Even the phrase, "mighty man of God," is a stretch. A truly mighty man of God, the Apostle Paul, would not boast of such a description. Recall Paul's words considering the spirits at war within him. "I know nothing good lives in me, that is, my sinful nature. For I have a desire to do what is good, but cannot carry it out. For what I do is not the good thing I want to do; no the evil I do not want to do – this I keep on doing" (Romans 7:19). These are not the words of a mighty man, particularly when Paul adds, "What a wretched man I am!"

From this humble point, Paul takes his surest steps towards becoming mighty. He wrote, "Who will set me free me free from the body of this death? Thanks be to God through Jesus Christ our Lord" (Romans 7: 24-25). When Paul is brought low through his weakness and failure, he leans totally upon Jesus, and claims as his only true wisdom, "to only know Christ and Him crucified" (I Corinthians 2:2). He becomes a mighty man of God, but not by virtue of his own might. Paul knows he is mighty only because his God is The Almighty.

Still, I believe Paul would never accept the description of himself as a mighty man of God. Describing himself as a "wretched man" and possessing a nature in which nothing good grows," Paul sought to become a real man of God. Like the Apostle Paul, my aim is not to be mighty, but simply to be real, to be authentic.

While confronting the wretched man I am, I've been told, "Paul, you think too much. You gotta' lower your standards. Just go shallow and then all this stuff won't bother you." One who is striving to be a real man of God can't "just go shallow," but there is an element of wisdom within the advice. It's valid to the degree it says, "Paul, stop beating your head against the wall for things which you'll never change. Stop trying to fix what is not yours to fix." In this sense, it encourages me to become more contented in life as it is, rather than striving for what I think is life should be.

However, the resolution of turmoil was not achieved by lowering my standards, or going "shallow," but by reconciling the standards I live by. The mental unrest was not a result of thinking too deeply, but derived from the Spirit's rebuke due to living according to conflicting sets of standards, living double-mindedly.

I don't believe the answer is to lower one's standards, or to pretend to be spiritually comatose. We will "serve one master, and hate the other" (Luke 16:13), or we'll suffer the spiritual turmoil of vainly trying to serve both. Within the notion of lowering one's standards, is veiled the decision to serve one master, demanding an answer to the question, "Which one?" If God is our standard, we can know His peace. If the Dark Angel is our choice, or if we simply choose to make no choice, the Dark Angel will delude us into believing we have found peace. Real peace of spirit and mind is making the choice, and making the right choice. Real peace is found only in walking with the Prince of Peace, Jesus.

At work, people viewed me as either very quiet, or as over-the-top gregarious with a viciously sarcastic tongue. (Either was a means of controlling my interactions with others.) They assumed when I was too quiet something was wrong, or if I was wildly sarcastic all was well, though the opposites were true. The sarcasm really meant I wasn't dealing well with darkness and anger. While I was trying to be a real man of God, I was far from it, losing out to the overflow of my heart, voiced as vicious humor.

So, how could I credibly be a real man of God at work? Coworkers had seen my angry side. Some while laughing saw through the dark colors of my words. How could a man who speaks in words of veiled hatred credibly share Christ with them?

To now strive to be a man of God presents the same challenge the scripture reveals for a man who will not be received as a prophet among his people, those who have seen both the good and the bad of him. The bad destroys any credibility and is nearly impossible to overcome in order to be a real testimony of the love and purposes of God.

Worse than destroying my credibility, I knew how far I was falling away from God's will each time my evil words revealed my sour heart. Far worse, I knew my angry words were, again, crucifying the Son of God and putting Him to an open shame (Hebrews 6:6). The guilt of putting Jesus to an open shame is a heavy indictment against one seeking a higher plane with God. There is a burden in secret sins,

MIGHTY OR REAL? ➤

knowing you've disappointed Jesus. It's quite a heavier burden to know your public sins are holding Jesus before the world in open and sorrowful shame.

How can a man who claims to love Jesus shame Him by careless, unloving words? The question reminds me of a four year old boy who was asked, "What does love mean?" His insightful reply was, "When someone loves you, the way they say your name is different. You just know your name is safe in their mouth."

If a little boy already understands that idea, it won't be long before he understands, "May the words of my mouth and the medita-tions of my heart be pleasing in Your sight, O, Lord" (Psalm 19:14). He'll soon know the power and the light which come from speaking Jesus' name and God's Truth in love. The sound of it in his mouth will be different, and safe.

Being a real man of God demands Jesus' knowing His name is safe in my mouth. With "safe" meaning the words I speak about Jesus are not contradicted by the way I act. Moving out of darkness demands I never hold Jesus to an open shame, always keeping His words and His name safe in my mouth.

The greater challenge may be from a different perspective. Jesus knows I have kept His name too safe in my mouth. His name is "safe," as in being locked away in a vault, far too seldom unlocked to speak His name. I may often sing, "I love to tell the story of Jesus and His love," but if I fail to tell the story, His name is too safe in my mouth.

I have more often been guilty of speaking in a way which shames Jesus, but recently I learned about the blessings I have missed by keeping his name too safe. The experience also highlighted the dou-ble-mindedness of men, who claim to be a child of God, but live as quite another child on the job.

I've known a man nearly twenty years through my work. Although his father is a minister, I always perceived this man, by the nature of our relationship, to be the wayward, faithless son. As our casual friendship developed through the years, it was one of very lighthearted jesting, and sometimes very coarse jesting.

Knowing his father is advanced in age, I asked him if his father was still preaching. He assured, "Oh, yes; he's eighty-eight years old and loves what he does. He'll never lay that down!" Then he continued, "I fill in preaching sometimes for him, too."

Those words hit me like a chill. How did this man with whom I had one kind of relationship, have a very different relationship with a group of people who receive him as a minister of the Word? Certainly, ministers are simply men, too, but we know from the Word that those who teach will be held to a higher standard before God. Indeed, they will be accountable for the souls they've led to Him, but are accountable even more for the souls they've led away from Him.

In a moment I faced the truth. We both sought to live for God, but were doing so as double-minded men. Neither of us was matching our Sunday words with our Monday through Saturday walk. Neither of us was living as men fully committed to God. Though we will always be sin-prone men, if we are truly His children, we are called to be all-or-nothing men; either hot or cold, never to be lukewarm or double-minded men.

In the vanity of double-mindedness, all hope of gaining the prize of Heaven is lost; the hope truly is in vain. "Being a double-minded man, unstable in all his ways, that man ought not to expect that he will receive anything from the Lord." (James 1:7-8)

The tenor of our relationship changed that day. We're still casual and comfortable friends, still jesting with each other, but now it's a different kind of kinship. Now, I hold him accountable to a higher standard, and he's testing me just the same. We know real men of God are not necessarily mighty men; neither can they be double-minded men.

Surely, within the new tenor of our friendship is the essence of the scripture telling us to, "encourage one another, and build up one another" (I Thessalonians 5:11). What a travesty it is that for twenty years neither of us said anything which would build up the other. Neither of us had spoken a word of praise to God. Neither of us had given a hint of our desire to be a real man of God. Now, holding each other accountable to The Light has been another blessing which helped me emotionally remain in Jesus' light. With the blessing comes the responsibility to help him remain in the Light. Thereby, I hold more to the Lord's purpose in this world, remaining in the light as He is in the Light. I thank God for the little blessings which, again and again, show me the Light.

When I mentioned to him we would have to change the tenor of our relationship, in his usual lighthearted manner he said, "Oh, no; I'm still the same old guy." In a sense, yes he is, but it is part of our responsibility to each other as real men of God to not let each other remain "the same old guy." After the duplicity of our lives was revealed, it is my responsibility to build him up in the cause for which he is called in Christ. I cannot let him continue as the same old guy. Certainly, Jesus did not die so we can persist in being the same old guys; guys who will continue to hold Christ to an open shame.

In the new relationship I remembered the admonition to "avoid worldly and empty chatter, for it will lead to further ungodliness" (II Timothy 2:6). Without a mind set on the things higher and nobler, the things of God, the course of idle chatter always leads downhill. By avoiding the coarse jesting of our past, it is a blessing to speak about higher things, and for each of us to live closer to being the men of God we are called to be.

The challenge of being a real man of God at work is in the confusion of perceptions of being a mighty man. Adding my real but introverted desire to control others, and my frustration in being unable to control them, the resulting stew of simmering emotions sometimes boiled over in anger and sarcasm.

Control is not always negative. It is necessary, even God ordained, when applied scripturally. But, for an unbalanced and controlling personality, the more things are out of control, the more absolutely control is sought. It's a self-defeating combination to be one who at almost any cost seeks to control others, but also strives to make no waves. The ironic combination results in passive/aggressive control.

When things are going well, the controller is passive. When things are only a little awry, the passive/aggression (more accurately, passive manipulation) kicks into gear. And, when things are really out of control, when frustrations build and emotions rage, passivity is subverted by anger. In the extreme, passive aggression becomes passive/abusive control when all thinking errors hold full sway. But, the self-condemning twist to my aggression was its inward direction.

In seeking to make no waves, I was most aggressive against myself; the errant thinking arrows pointed inwardly. As the thinking errors reigned, the deep darkness took its own aggressive and abusive control.

Finally, my urge for control was trumped by situations in which I held no control. There were situations in which I held some sway when my son was a teenager. In his present circumstance, I could only find peace by forfeiting any vague illusion of control. By admitting I was powerless, by not tackling matters too difficult for me, I began to find peace.

Control is often grossly mistaken for leadership, and leadership is often mistaken for being mighty. Part of my pursuit towards higher ground meant giving up my desire for control, and giving up the perceived might of leadership.

Those struggling against thinking errors tend to obsess over the trivial matters because we feel powerless to affect weightier matters. We seek to control what we shouldn't, while ignoring what we should control – the essence of seeing "the speck that is in your brother's eye, but do not notice the log that is in your own eye" (Luke 6:41). Focusing on my eyesight was the beginning of giving up control. It is the beginning of forfeiting my self-appointed role as police and prosecutor, judge and jury.

Quite an amazing thing happened as I loosened my desire to lead by controlling. When I backed down from making every decision for those I managed, they stepped up to the opportunities to lead. They thrived in some measure of their own control, and I thrived by giving up the burden of control. I relished the change because it freed my mind to think more about the things above, and to focus on the renewing of my mind.

Giving up control was certainly not an original idea of mine. Jesus, the consummate leader, modeled the plan first. Though Jesus had no weakness of His own, He did not lead by controlling others. Knowing He needed to develop leaders to carry on the purposes of God in this world, He led by developing others to take control of His mission. Jesus chose a ragtag group of men of no high calling among the religious elite. Jesus left the leadership not to mighty men, but real men according to His making.

In the world's wisdom, the judgments about the worth of men are turned wrong side out, compared to the biblical model. Men who do only what they are duty-bound and sworn to do are exalted as heroes. But, those who are truly exemplary in leadership, service, or vision are picked apart until they are scorned in an open shame. Men who achieve great things based on the wisdom of man are held up as visionaries, while men who labor to fulfill God's will, are denigrated as narrow minded, intolerant, and out of bounds by shining the light of Truth into the darkness of man's wisdom.

Paul, in the opening chapters of I Corinthians, refutes man's wisdom. Men of this world hold their own learned wisdom highest, though the wisdom of man is foolishness before God. As Paul rhetorically poses, "If anything of God is foolish, even that foolishness is above the highest wisdom of man." A real man of God holds an attitude like Paul's, as we often sing, "Forbid it, Lord, that I should boast, save in the death of Christ my Lord." A real man of God remembers, "Let no man deceive himself. If any thinks that he is wise, he must become foolish so that he may become wise" (I Corinthians 3:18). Therefore, just as it is written, "Let him who boasts, boast in the Lord" (I Corinthians 1:31).

Men are considered mighty not in the worth of their work, but in the value of the things acquired from their income; the acquisition of big-boys' toys. Too often, to appear as mighty men we spend money we don't have on things we don't need. In the striving to pay for and maintain these toys, there's little room to be a mighty man of God. Becoming a real man of God mandates not striving for the toys of this world. In the striving we are trying to serve two masters, God and materialism, and in the striving we fail to serve The Master.

If one obtains all the seemingly must-have possessions, or is discontent because he can't, envy and greed-fed depression can be the sad reward. Depression is the by-product of being seduced into the world's mindset to look right, drive the right mega-truck, and live in the right house with all the toys. We are so overloaded by the striving for the toys of this world we have no time to live as distinct from the world. Loaded with the burdens of things which fade away, our lives consumed to support them, how is there time to be real men of God?

God does not require asceticism, unless the materialism gets in the way. Then, like the parable of the rich man, we may be challenged to sell all that we have. In balance, we should long for the things above more than the things of this world. May we thirst for God rather than thirst for things. By resolving to thirst for Him we move closer to becoming real men of God.

The failing of measuring a man by his possessions is evidenced in those we seek as leaders in the church. We lose sight of their spiritual worthiness by assessing their financial worth. How rare it is to see an appointed leader who is still employed in a modest, blue collar job, or whose plain-Jane car is ten years old. (I know of only one.) Such a man is likely judged as not having well managed his personal affairs and his ability to lead the church is suspect. Rather, he may manage far better than most men by virtue of his limited income. And, he may have more of a heart for "the least of these" among us.

Which is the better ideal of being a mighty man of God – rich in possessions, or wealthy in Spirit? Only the latter, a man wealthy in Spirit, is a real man of God. God's purposes may yet be much better served by a similar ragtag group of men as the apostles, unshackled by great possessions.

From a friend's blog, I believe this truth about the real men of God in the church. "The church will not thrive by virtue of perfect leaders, but by the virtue of wounded leaders revealing a perfect Savior." Wounded leaders know their continuing need for redemption has nothing to do with their possessions or power.

Overcoming my past failures as a Christian at work may prove a larger challenge than overcoming my darkness. Every day I must purpose to do three things. I must strive to let people see more of Jesus in me, in both the way I lead and in the way I follow. I must "guard my ways that I may not sin with my tongue; I will guard my mouth as with a muzzle" (Psalm 39:1). I must be sure God's Word and His name are safe in my mouth, both in what I say and by what I won't say, "putting away all abusive speech," until all the utterances of my mouth are in righteousness (and) there is nothing crooked or perverted in them" (Colossians 3:8, Proverbs 8:8). Surely, I must rely upon Jesus to help me, for if the Apostle Paul couldn't rely upon his own strength, I can't either.

Relying upon Jesus to help me, the ultimate goal of becoming a real man of God is attaining the promised glories of Heaven, becoming a citizen of the eternal Zion. My tongue and the past stores of my heart shook my assurance of Heaven. I remember David's words, "O Lord, who may abide in Your tent? Who may dwell on Your holy hill? He who walks with integrity," not as a double-minded man, "and who works righteousness, and speaks truth in his heart, he does not slander with his tongue...he who does these things will never be shaken" (Psalm15:1-3, 5).

Real, or mighty - the goal of either word is to become authentic, having no alloy of wills or values, becoming an honest and single-minded man of God. Being authentic is when I am able to remove the Sunday mask on Monday morning, and the face and character behind the mask are the same. Being authentic is revealing my strengths, and if it serves the cause of Christ, to also reveal my failings as a means to reveal His power in working all things for good.

Being a real or mighty man of God requires equal measures of two ingredients – passion and compassion; passion for the Truth, and compassion for leading others to the Truth. As men exercise both passion and compassion, we become mighty men of God, by declaring not our strengths, but by declaring our dependence upon Him. We are mighty not by celebrating our victories, but rejoicing in Jesus' help through our times of weakness.

So, which will it be – real, or mighty? I'll aim for real, and if God so wills, I'll depend upon Him to make me mighty. Besides, I can wait for "mighty" until that day when I join the mighty chorus singing a new song with the redeemed of all the ages. Indeed, that will be both real and mighty!

NINE

STEPPING STONES

From a young age, circus elephants are restrained by a chain around one foot. The chain is secured by a heavy stake driven deep into the ground. As the elephant becomes accustomed to straining against the stake without escaping, he stops trying. Soon the chain alone without the stake is enough restraint. The animal could flee at will, but has lost the will. The elephant is bound by the memories of restraint.

Persistent depression is a heavy chain. One may pull against the chain, perhaps loosening the stake, but if not overcome, depression becomes the defining restraint of life. The experiences of depression become the restraining memory. I almost forgot how to strain against the chain.

The deepest darkness, the suicidal struggles, returned twice through the years. The hopelessness was defining my life. The final decision was never made, but the words of the final note were. This degree of darkness restrained me from stepping out for any purpose; neither for Christ or my career.

Still, through the decades, I was tethered to a measure of hope through the calling of Christ, though I did not submit to the calling. I was bound to Him by the blessings of songs; the only expression of my feeble faith. Yet, a few songs were enough for God to work through to accomplish His will. By those songs He never let me completely forget how to pull against the chain.

Again, in the words of *Higher Ground,* I sensed the urge to pull one more time, to pull really hard against depression's chain. In ways which I could not comprehend at the beginning, these words framed the effort and voiced the prayer through which I finally broke the chains.

> *I want to live above the world,*
> *Where Satan's darts at me are hurled;*
> *For faith has caught the joyful sound,*
> *The song of saints on higher ground.*
>
> *Lord lift me up and let me stand,*
> *By faith on Heaven's table land.*
> *A higher plane than I have found,*
> *Lord plant my feet on higher ground.*

Have you ever traveled a very long distance, weary after driving far too many miles? Reaching your destination, perhaps you wondered how you made it? In the fatigue, you couldn't recall landmarks along the way. You could only marvel that you made it safely home.

The transition from darkness into the light is not one of those journeys. It can't be. It requires an awareness of every challenge which must be overcome, though at the start one may not know each challenge. It is not a trip which can be totally preplanned. Once started, twists and turns will become obvious and each one must be traveled. Nearing the destination as best I know it now; it is a blessing to remember each mile of the way. Each was a stepping stone towards the light. Originally, I only sought a light to overwhelm the darkness. What I found is the True Light, the light of Christ.

Despite the decades-long frustrations of trying to chart my course, I didn't plan the beginning of this transition. I was pursuing change, but God was proving I wasn't ready for the change. His plan for me worked in ways I couldn't plan. I could not have foreseen the factors which would concur to lead me out of my darkness. By the unexpected turns in the journey, He was teaching me His ways are higher than my ways.

His higher ways included teaching me about real faith, prayer, and the need to trust Him. While seeking my way, I was trying to force change which would not come. In my growing exasperation,

God taught me I was striving for the wrong change and the wrong light. I learned that until I found contentment in my present circumstances, I would find no contentment in the changes I was forcing.

Through my glass-half-empty nature, and within the emotional chaos of stalled plans, old wounds, and my son's incarceration, I was drawing closer to seeking the light by different means. Hearing the simple message, "failure is not final," and being asked to speak about being a mighty man of God, circumstances in my life were working together to begin the transition to the light.

More accurately, those circumstances were not conspiring to change me. God's working through those situations finally led me to say, "Okay, God, I'll do it your way." This was the first and most important stepping stone; the step which cleared the way for the renewing of my mind. The renewal I sought was for the Spirit's regeneration which is promised to all who seek Him. In my past persistence of relying on my spirit, I made no room for the Holy Spirit's working. The joy which should belong to one born again "of water and the Spirit" could not be realized, for by the thinking patterns which built the high walls of my darkness, I ignored the Spirit. I had to get my spirit out of the way for His Spirit to bring light to my soul.

When I knew there had to be a better way, and committed to finding it according to God's plan, I had to pursue means never before considered. The Spirit worked through unexpected people, unexpected challenges, and unexpected spiritual reality checks along the way. Learning to accept His unexpected ways was crucial to my transition.

In a earlier period of toxic anxieties and frustrations, I found encouragement from a young man still living in the small Texas town where I lived as a child. His was a life I had often viewed as unlikely to achieve much, but I came to see him in a much different light.

He was the middle of three sons from the best-known family in town. The older brother was the star of the town; more so after his untimely death. The younger brother was arguably more handsome than God should allow. But, there was this middle child, morbidly obese, and too dyslexic finish a college degree. He lived at home until his thirties, holding a succession of so-so jobs. He was the son whose exploits would likely be the shortest paragraph in a Christmas newsletter.

However, he possessed an endearing and special gift – a true compassion for people, particularly an affinity and affection for the elderly. This quality suited him for a new career. He began selling medical supplies – canes and crutches, walkers and wheelchairs, and the like. He loved the job, and I can imagine his customers loved him.

His employer sought to hire a thirteen-state, regional sales manager, and he purposed to get the job. Many people told him, "You'll never get that job – there's no way you're qualified for it! They'll demand a college degree; they'll demand years of successful management experience. They'll demand someone who, well, someone who looks the part!"

The dissuasion didn't deter him. He went for it with all his heart. His enthusiasm, his compassion and his determination won. He landed the job, and he is soaring in success!

I love his story. It is about a flawed man breaking through his memories of past failures, breaking through a self-defeating mindset, and breaking his restraining chains. His breakthroughs were much like those I sought. While God has proven He has different plans for me, through this young man He was also proving His working in all things for good.

In the overcoming of obstacles to find the light, I had to depend on others. Either by their example or by their direct involvement in my life, I knew the depression and phobias could not be overcome alone. God's establishment of the marriage relationship and the establishment of His church prove He never intended for anyone to struggle alone.

In the fits and starts of overcoming depression, most of the failings were mine, but some of the failings were of others. It was hard to find the right person, the one who cared enough, with empathy rather than sympathy. And, the person who loved me in spite of the awful truths; who was supportive, but more so, would bluntly confront my thinking. This was a tricky proposition, but was another crucial step.

Much of my difficulty in finding the person derives from the nature of friendships between men. I remember longing for a deep friendship, like the friendships my wife enjoys which have endured through the years and over thousands of miles.

Not long after a cross-country move, we met a family with whom we were instantly friends. I found in the husband so many things to share, and I was thrilled by this nascent friendship. While on an overnight hunting trip, knowing he struggled with similar issues, I opened up with him in a way I rarely had. By the time we'd driven home the next day, he had emotionally vacated the friendship. We remained friends, but it is seldom closer than an arm's length.

Perhaps, the difficulty in men being supportive of other men is in the way we are socialized. We are to maintain control in emotional situations, never vulnerable to others' emotions. The 'beast' will not be controlled by the interplay of emotions.

It is like being around cattle on my great-grandfather's farm. A bull may approach out of curiosity, the expectation of food, or to let you scratch his head. But, if you grab its horns, it will forcefully jerk its head to wrest free of your grip. He will step back several strides and stand broadside, distrusting and ready to bolt. Men are just like ornery bulls – in the horn of a problem, don't let anyone else take control.

Finding the right person will likely not come from within one's close family. It's not because their love isn't deep enough, or their desire to help isn't true. Often, the pain is just too close to them, also. For them, it may be like the same misgivings I had in helping my sons; not sure of the best way to love them, or which way they would receive the love I could give. Perhaps, those closest to the one in need are hoping against hope, trying not to see what is plain to see.

For those long involved in the church, there is an assumption to confide in and seek guidance from a minister. By my experience, a minister is unlikely to be a wholly willing advocate. The obstacle is his larger responsibility to the corporate body – both spiritually and, sadly, politically. Likely, he cannot invest so deeply into one person.

However, I believe the problem is rooted, again, in men's perceptions of power. Ministering to others in their deepest struggles, requires identifying with and having an empathy with their darkness, which implies a weakness in him. The empathy is an obstacle to maintaining the appearance of power, and of being above such darkness. Any appearance of having known his own darkness is believed to compromise the veracity of his faith and his strengths in leadership.

If I am misunderstanding this aspect of pastoral leadership, it is due to my first efforts to overcome my darkness. Over twenty years ago I sought the counsel of a minister in the Lord's church who is also a professional psychologist, highly respected and loved by many people. After meeting with him for several weeks, we finally ventured into the turbulent waters of the past. I remember the morning I told him my story; one which had never been told. It was the first time I tried to tell childhood experiences which still riled the emotional waters of my life.

He sat quietly until I finished. For several moments he studied me. It was hard for me to judge his thoughts. Then, without inflection or emotion, he raised his brows and dead-panned, "Is that all that's bothering you?"

I was dumbfounded, thinking only, "Damn you, man, I just poured out my guts; all the crap and darkness, and then you say, 'Is that all?'" As I left, I was developing a slow-burning anger. Before long, I was seething mad and wounded. The trust I invested in him was violated. I felt like the bull on my grandpa's farm. He had grabbed me by the horns. I had to wrest free.

I don't know the counselor's plans beyond that day, how he may have counseled me towards rebalancing my mind. I didn't see him again. I couldn't handle the question, "Is that all that's bothering you?" And, I spent more than twenty years insulted by the first counseling experience. At almost any time, I could still stir the resentment against this man. From a counseling perspective, I don't know if his words were the start of an appropriate remedy. Perhaps, others would have responded differently. But, finally I began to see a more balanced perspective of that day, derived from the stepping stones I have now followed towards the light.

My anger with the minister passed with a new understanding that he was not minimizing my experiences. He already knew my pattern of thinking in all-or-nothing terms. He knew my subjective reasoning always trumped objectivity. I believe he intended to help me look beyond my darkness, to look beyond the horizon and see the Light.

But, it was more than that. I believe he was beginning to tell me much more, though speaking carefully. If he had spoken plainly in the words I understand now, his words would have been rejected by the sour soil of my mind. I could not understand; the truth was more than I would accept.

He was beginning to teach me the healing truth. God's love is big enough, His mercy is deep enough, and His grace is more than sufficient to meet my needs. Like the crowd fed by two fishes and five loaves, by a full measure of His provision for my healing, I can feast to the full with much to spare.

Just as I replaced old thinking patterns with new, I had to replace old habits. It required saying "yes" to opportunities and challenges which I'd avoided by a habitual and inflexible "No." In many ways, I had to prepare to say "Yes," particularly to becoming the kind of friend I was seeking for myself.

My wife seems always to be a person in whom others securely confide their cares and burdens. Many times though I have asked her, "Why are you borrowing their trouble?"

She always replies, "I'm not borrowing trouble; I'm just trying to help." And, help she does.

In the blessings of my renewal, as I began to walk in the Light, it was impossible not to talk about. The situations in which it flowed naturally seemed often to be with someone also in need. Telling my story opened the door for others to tell theirs. And, it didn't at all feel like I was borrowing trouble. It was proof - to live in the Light, one must share the Light.

In the willingness to be open and supportive of others, I learned about what I call, the blessings of wet feet. God waits for us to act upon our faith, in a sense to step in the water before He blesses us. Like the Israelites who had to trust in God to cross the Jordan River, I had to be willing to step into the water. The blessings in wet feet derived from stepping into the troubled waters of others' lives, or stepping out by faith in whatever He wills.

In God's time I found the right person, actually more than one.

I found these people not by seeking someone to meet my need, but by stepping out to be the kind of friend I was seeking. When beginning to find my light, I tried to help another person find hers, or tried to help another parent suffering from the incarceration of her son, I found the right people.

This step proved ironic. The stepping stone was not in finding a supportive and abiding confidant for me; rather, it was becoming a confidant to someone else. Now, as each of us supports the other, we can share a laugh or a tear. We can be the counselor or the counselee. We can say tender words without being weak, or say "crazy" words without being condemned. Either way, we shine light into each other's darkness.

Though beginning this introspection still burdened and angry with the first counselor, I now see my burdens within the broader range of tragedies which beset man. Perhaps, in some way, his counselor's question, "Is that all?" was justifiable. Admitting that helped me realize I had moved from darkness into the Light. God answered my prayers and is answering them still. God said if I would cast my burdens on the Lord, I could leave them all behind. Why did it take me thirty years to trust this? I have no explanation other than it took that long to finally stop depending on myself and start to depend on Him; to grow in the trust to leave my cares behind, and to believe in His "all things for good."

It's been three years since I decided to pursue God's way. Through persistence in the decision, I found the Light. Before, even as I began this book, I didn't trust God's ways are big enough. Trust was a work in progress until the day I wrote the chapter, *Vested in Truth.* I believe the Holy Spirit, as my Comforter, helped me accept Truth as I invested more of His Word into my life. By gradual acceptance through my steadily warming faith, I was able to comprehend more of the Truth. This measure of assurance in God's working was a huge leap across stepping stones.

Recalling my decision to discontinue counseling with that minister, I perpetuated an old habit of fleeing. I did not persevere though a perceived adversity. I cut and ran at the first slap of opposition, in a rash of thinking errors and the expectation of failure. The Apostle

Paul would have told me, "Press on to the prize." Churchill would have said, "Never give up!" But, I didn't press on; I did give up the fight. Good intentions died in resignation, just like the Israelites who turned back to remain in bondage.

I recall playing Little League baseball with my older brother, Ben. He was little (Dad often called him "Peewee".), but he could really play the game. One typical, hot and humid Texas evening, Ben, while up to bat, taught me a lighthearted lesson about persevering through adversity.

On the first pitch, Ben hit a towering shot which drifted foul down the left field line. Second pitch, just the same; quickly he was behind in the count, 0 and 2. Third pitch the same – a long, high shot, foul down the line. The fourth pitch, fifth pitch, were the same, except now the crowd was really getting into it. Sixth pitch; yes, it was the same. The pitcher kept pitching and Ben kept swinging, but not yet in synch. Seventh, eighth, and ninth pitches – all resulted in the same long, foul hits. On pitch ten – finally a hot-pepper grounder skipped past the third baseman and Ben scrambled to first.

Okay, like the movies, it would be a better story if he had powered the ball over the center field fence. But this is not the *Field of Dreams*; this is reality. The lesson was about persevering – Ben just kept swinging until he got it right.

I remember fondly the countless hours my Dad spent practicing baseball with me in our front yard. I'm not sure how he made the time for all the practicing, but he with great patience and encouragement helped me play baseball, though I never amounted to much of a player. Frankly, I don't think there was any real spark of talent revealed in all the hours of practice, but practice we did.

Now, I don't at all believe Dad's first goal was to teach baseball. Dad was generously investing himself into my life. Amid the trials and darkness in his own life, he was giving of his life to build mine. The teaching was not how to power a home run over the centerfield fence. In Dad's way, without the words which were likely too hard to say, he was telling me how to deal with life. In baseball lingo, he was saying, "Paul, step up to the plate, keep your eye on the ball, and just keep swinging." If it was the only lesson he taught me, it would have been enough.

I waited too many years to heed his lesson, but finally I did step up and persevere, and with Christ's leading began winning over the darkness. Through Christ I had, and still have, a bigger bat and I just kept swinging.

Many of the stepping stones along this path I chose, but it was by my investment in His Word and the leading of the Spirit those steps were successful. I chose to become vested in Truth. I chose to audit my relationship with God, including the foundational issue of confidence in my salvation. I chose to depend on His promise to work all things for good, and to develop a vital relationship with Him through prayer. As I persevered in each step, the Spirit revealed the worth of that step.

I also chose to make peace – to be peaceable with the past, more content with the present, and more trusting for the future. The decision to be peaceable sounds easier than it proved to be. Living peaceably (still a work in progress) was primarily a decision to live humbly. In conflict with anyone, the desire to be peaceable required of me to get past believing I deserve to be right; believing I deserve to win. Living peaceably demanded forfeiting my assumed right to be proven better than another – even those who hurt me deeply.

It required, and I am trying, being peaceable with self. For a man who likes control, but so often has lived in some ways out of control, making peace with me was a challenge. I released the disappointments in the goals I planned but didn't pursue, and the goals I pursued but failed. The season for those things passed, and in the desire for peace, I accepted the passing. It's now a matter of not taking me too seriously. Not lowering the bar, but when I don't meet the bar, accepting that it's alright – believing that failure really is not final.

Unless someone is either wrongly exerting their will over me in a way which contradicts the will of God, or if they are open to hear the Truth of God, I have no inherent right to expect them to live by my standards. Again, if they are seeking, I must be ready to give an account of God's Truth, but living peaceably requires not thinking more highly of myself than I aught, or demanding others to accept my beliefs.

I've long remembered one of the most peaceful feelings I ever enjoyed, while vacationing in the mountains of Colorado in 1978. One very brisk morning in early October, I stood in Glacier Basin of Rocky Mountain National Park; a Texas flatlander, awed by the beautiful mountains around me.

All the recent TV news reporting focused on the meetings hosted by Jimmy Carter, with Menachim Begin and Anwar Sadat, in an effort to broker a Middle East peace treaty. Amid the negotiations and expectations of a real breakthrough, the highest anticipation concerned whether or not Prime Minister Begin and President Sadat would shake hands. Beyond the words of a treaty, people wanted to see them reach across their vast gulf of ideologies to shake hands.

As I stood alone that morning, gazing at the wonders around me, and a sensing the Master who created it all, I thought, "In the whole scheme of things it doesn't matter what happens at Camp David." In the vast scope of creation, and as time has proven, it mattered very little what happened there.

I needed to apply the same thoughts to being peaceable with myself. The things I now try to do, whether I succeed or fail, in the broad sweep of His world, matter very little. The greater will and the purposes of God will be accomplished in some small way because of, or in spite of anything I do.

Seeking to be a real man of God requires being a peaceable man. In striving to be more like Jesus, I must remember to ask myself, "Who is Jesus is if He is not a man of peace?" His peace truly does matter.

While living with an unbalanced mindset, I rejected the notion my illness was due to a lack of faith. To anyone who dared to imply that, I thought, "You just don't understand." I was the one who didn't understand. I finally saw my persistent emotional imbalance was not caused by childhood experiences, the tragedies of life, or by the sins of others. Overcoming my faltering faith, I admitted my depression was the fruit of my own persistent sins. The illness was a consequence of sin, and the depression itself became sinful. If anyone had dared to tell me, "Paul, you need to repent of your sins in order to resolve your depression," they'd been in for a fight.

Avoiding the all-or-nothing thinking error, I won't say all mental illness is sin, or say anyone's illness is wholly a consequence of sin. Neither will I say one's nature to be anxious, melancholy, or depressed is sinful. Certainly, my illness was rooted in a genetic propensity for emotional illness and is still a fruit of physiological causes. Amid the range of factors, depression is a continuing consequence of the original sin upon my basic nature. The experiential factors of which I had no control are not my sin; however, my responses to those experiences became my sin. We all face temptations to sin – I submitted to the temptation by submitting to the persistent darkness.

Intransigent darkness, unlike situational depression, is born from and nurtured in sin. My depression became sin when I did not trust God to heal my mind. Without understanding it at the time, I was saying, "God, You made me, but You can't fix me." Years ago when I chose to label myself as 'crazy,' I was really saying to God, "I don't accept the promises of Your Word, I won't accept Your Spirit to comfort me. I won't accept the examples of Jesus and the apostles to renew my mind." It became sin when I chose to settle for an angry, unbalanced mind.

Is there a more certain recipe for living with a broken spirit, extreme thinking, and depression? One who understands the depravity of his life, and knows of his estrangement from God, but does not seek Christ for healing has no hope. Indeed, when I listened to a deceitful voice within and settled for the lie, "You can't fix me," I forfeited any real hope.

How could I expect to be delivered from my darkness if I didn't acknowledge the source of my darkness – sin? Remembering the wise proverb, "He who conceals his transgressions will not prosper, but he who confesses and forsakes them will find compassion" (Proverbs 28:13). Not concealing my transgressions required my not concealing anything. Complete healing requires specific healing. I did not find healing, emotional balance and the renewing of my mind without treating the specific wounds and sins. I had to peel back the emotional scabs which may looked like past healing, but still hid wounds, sins, and darkness.

To persist in my darkness would continue to be sinful as it violates Paul's exhortation to, "put on the Lord Jesus Christ, and make no provision for the flesh in regard to its lusts" (Romans 13:14). In emotional darkness, whether the result of extreme thinking errors or the cyclical thoughts which spiral downward into sin, depressive thoughts make every provision for the flesh. "He has ceased to be wise and to do good. He plans wickedness upon his bed; he sets himself on a path that is not good; he does not despise evil" (Psalm 36:3-4). Before any other action towards sin is pursued, the decision to remain in darkness makes accommodation for the thoughts which permit rationalizations for sin. Before there is any physical provision for sin there is always mental accommodation for sinning.

In the days when I was acting sinfully and justifying it by thinking, "I know I'm being a monster and just can't help it," I was rejecting the Spirit's power to renew my mind. In the rejection of His power to heal, I was giving myself permission to persist in sin. By accepting the depression I allowed myself to live in ways defined by the depression. I allowed myself to make every provision for the flesh.

In the audit of my faith and my mindset, I understood the sins which derived from depression, and the depression itself, were all in my spiritual debits column. Then I began to more fully see the need for Jesus in my assets column, and the need to repent for every thought which made provision for sin. The resulting rebalanced mindset was the sum of a renewed spiritual balance sheet. By God's grace, Christ's redemption and the Spirit's renewal all spiritual debits are erased.

Now, in balance, I believe most people (certainly there are valid exceptions) can choose their emotions – at least their emotional reactions. We choose our thinking patterns. We choose who or what will be our master. And, within a heart which is not continually seeking the Lord's way, we choose which temptations to suborn unto sin.

Joseph lived victoriously despite the evil perpetrated against him, and in spite of the lurid temptations before him. He knew sin would separate him from inward peace, and from the victory which God purposed for him. Joseph's emotional balance held fast because he resisted temptation, making no provision for the flesh.

The penitential psalms of David are from a heart which knows his deepest sorrows are not from the assaults of his enemies. His utter despair is from the assault of his sins against God, and against his heart after God's heart (Acts 13:22).

David, when freed of his thinking errors, is not blaming any circumstance around his life for his sin when he writes, "There is no health in my bones because of my sin. For my iniquities are gone over my head; as a heavy burden they weigh too much for me" (Psalm 38:3-4). Then, David sings for the joy of his deliverance from his sins; "He brought me up out of the pit of destruction, out of the miry clay. And He set my feet upon a rock making my footsteps firm. He put a new song in my mouth, a song of praise to our God" (Psalm 40:2-3). David knew his deepest despair was of his own sinful making.

I, like David, had to acknowledge my sins before I could be delivered from their burden. "When I kept silent about my sin, my body wasted away through my groaning all day long. For day and night Your hand was heavy upon me; my vitality was drained away as with the fever heat of summer. I acknowledged my sin to You, and my sin I did not hide; I said, 'I will confess my transgressions to the Lord'; and you forgave the guilt of my sin" (Psalm 32:3-5). I had to know I could not find light without acknowledging my illness, my "groaning all day long" was primarily the consequence of my sins.

If I adopt a secular view of my depression, the mental strife is not sinful, or a result of sin. Cognitive therapies often focus on emotional illness as a product of experiences, separate from any association with personal guilt. However, as a Christian I am accountable to His standard. My illness was sin as long as I rejected His power for the renewing of my mind. I can't claim to be a Christian, but only rely upon Christ for salvation. I must account for sins by the measures of His Word. Otherwise, by using another standard for the accounting of my actions and illness, I would continue to live in as a double-minded man.

In the early days of introspection, there were many scriptures I didn't fully believe. My surest confidence in the renewal of my mind is a renewed trust in the scriptures I often doubted. Through the pressing on to higher ground, on each new plane the essence of a scripture was made known to me. Each revelation proves the worth of each step I have taken.

Amid the days of writing this chapter, I awoke in the night, and in the mornings, to a doubting mindset. While knowing I have been so blessed in this transition from darkness to the light, I doubted the worth of penning any account of the blessings. First, I considered the doubts were from the Dark Angel, subverting my spiritual growth. Then I wondered if my worry was tinged with new depression, yet I felt a measure of real contentment which made it difficult to even recall the darkness. While I wanted to tell of His leading me out of darkness, it felt like there was too little darkness to have mattered.

Then I realized what had happened. Already, by His healing He was taking away the pain from the past, removing its weight, and freeing my spirit. The things which for so many years riled the waters of troubling memories, now were made calm, the gulf was stilled.

Until recently I viewed the Spirit's working in all things for good externally, with myself as an onlooker. I considered His working in the situations around my life, as if solving the problems around me somehow was His ultimate purpose. Rather, the needful situations around my life were resolved so I could internalize His will for me. The darkness was resolved by Him not for external joy, but for internal peace. He revealed His working externally, in situations outside of my life, so I would be receptive to His working and His light within me. True Light does not derive from His orchestration of events around me, but from His re-orchestration of the mind within me.

Having renewed my mind and my thinking patterns, I have given up my self-labeling, "Depressed." Rather than describing myself as depressed, I now think of depression as a characteristic of my life, not as the controlling condition or as my identity.

That's no small distinction for it allowed the redefining of the goals for my life. I failed in the past yearnings to be free from the darkness because the valid goal had not been defined. My former plans were insufficient to bring me to the light. Those goals failed for being made in darkness, and being as fallible as the moods from which they were born.

My victory over darkness could only be achieved by accepting Jesus' purposes and leading. It required setting my definition of light in the transcendent, fixed, and immutable hope of His Word, focused on the promised glories of Heaven. Only when the goal was in the fixed and higher purposes of God would the transition to the light, which is His light, be won.

In the calling to be a soldier of the cross, in my past self-labeling, the uniform I wore bore several stripes. The first three stripes ranked me as a "depressed," "husband/father," and "Christian." Sadly, I wore the depressed stripe as my highest rank; if not by allegiance, by the reality of every duty being ordered through depression. By not having my duty defined through the commands of God, I became an insubordinate and wounded soldier.

Giving up the stripe of depression was very much like being busted back to buck private. The supposed privileges of self-direction are forfeited when a 'soldier' submits to the leading of Jesus. What was known had to be retrained in accordance to new marching orders.

Many, like me, have lived our lives with the stripes of a prisoner; stripes we wear for the mistakes of our own making. We are like prisoners constrained by our self-directed wills, trying time after time, stripe after stripe, to heal ourselves. This world tells us we can depend on material gain, becoming mighty and self-fulfilled. But, we must turn our eyes upon Jesus, fixing our eyes on His healing sacrifice, and the stripes He bore in our stead.

The scripture tells us, "By His stripes we are healed," but an insubordinate Christian does not trust the promise. In trying to heal our stripes alone, we are much like those who mourn and wail, beating themselves with rods. The 'rods' derive from an imbalanced mind, burdened by darkness, failure and guilt. No amount of self-flagellation will heal our minds. But, within the vast stores of God's blessings, we are healed by the all-sufficiency of Jesus. I finally accepted His healing and forfeited depression's stripes.

While depression is not the defining stripe of my life, it remains a characteristic of my life, and I accept it as a continuing thorn in the flesh. Ironically, while striving through Christ to move from my darkness, I accept it may be within God's will for me to know some depression as my thorn in the flesh.

However, I am cautious in ascribing my thorn to God. The

Apostle Paul's thorn was given by God as a means to prevent Paul from exalting himself because of the surpassing greatness of the revelation he received. On the other hand, my mental imbalance was not a gift from God, but largely the result of my sin, the work of the Dark Angel. Still, the recollection of the illness and, now and then, a few dark days can be used by God.

This sounds like Jesus failed to meet my needs, or that I received so much less than I sought in Him. Actually, I received much more than I sought. I gained a greater assurance of my faith. I gained a vision of my higher purposes, and a vision of the Spirit's working in all things for good. I gained the experience of His healing and a portion of His wisdom to help me overcome the darkness in the future. I hold to the promise of Jesus' leading through any darkness or trial.

Within the greater assurance of my faith, I treasure the words, "Now faith is the evidence of things hoped for, [the things earnestly expected] the conviction of things not seen" (Hebrews 11:1). The central import of these words is of faith as the guarantee of Heaven for which we yearn, but cannot see. Beyond this meaning, the verse bears upon many of my hopes, my earnest expectations. I hoped to find light for my life, and to find hope itself. As I invested in my faith, it became the medium and the guarantor of my hope. Like Heaven will be, the light I found had been unseen, but now is more than my eyes, or ears, or thoughts imagined.

When beginning to live in The Light, I reached a steep and humbling step. Reaching the next higher plane required a step downward – a step in humility. By the story of the Israelites' bondage to the Egyptians, I realized their story applies to anyone held captive – as slaves to another, slaves to sin, or slaves to darkness. Their story is my story.

They were bound by their lack of faith. Their deliverance was assured if their faith was sufficient to sustain their steps. God promised, yet they doubted. God provided, and still they doubted. God purposed; still they were resigned to failure. It was humbling to see my bondage to emotional darkness paralleled their bondage. Having been so weak of faith I, too, was resigned to failure.

Finally, overcoming the failings of my faith was the step to a higher plane. One day I sensed and expected a new understanding of this transition in my life. As I celebrated God's presence in my life by singing, it was a day in which a richer understanding of His Word was realized.

In a mindset now renewed and balanced, the mountains which had cast such long shadows across my life now seem to cast nearly none. Having crossed those mountains and looking back, they looked like mere swells on the horizon. I could still name each mountain, but I could no longer force the feelings of bearing their immense burdens. I could not force the shadow of any mountain to darken my mind.

In a moment, one of those wonderful, then-sings-my-soul moments, I understood the words, "Truly I say to you, if you have the faith the size of a mustard seed, you will say to this mountain, 'Move from here to there,' and it will move; and nothing will be impossible to you" (Matthew 17:20).

YES, THEN SINGS MY SOUL! MY MOUNTAINS MOVED! THIS IS LIGHT! THIS IS PEACE! THIS IS THE VICTORY OF FAITH!

Surely, every step by His leading has been a blessing. Every step strengthened my stride for pressing onward. This latest step was to the sweetest plane, when looking back I saw the mountains indeed had moved by faith in Him. But, these last two steps were not of my choosing. They were steps I could not foresee, for they were turns in the journey of God's choosing. (Did you see what was happening better than I saw it coming?)

First, I saw myself as being no different than the Israelites in slavery. Now, I've proclaimed victory through faith which moved my mountains. For years I bristled at anyone who dared say a lack of faith prevented me from overcoming depression. Now, I have proven them to be right. Faith is the surest stepping stone from darkness into His light.

Certainly, faith is not the lone answer. In the range of physiological, experiential, and emotional factors causing mental illnesses, much more than faith is needful and valid. Much more than faith can be used by the Spirit in His working through all things for good. I've had some counseling and I've depended on medication for many years. Finally, I've depended on faith for my complete renewal through Jesus and in the healing powers of God. The counseling taught me some strategies. The medicine kept my head above the waves, but medicine only superficially balances one's mind; it does not resolve anything. It was my faith which finally brought me safely to the life-as-it-should-be shore. If I could only have one treatment, I'll take faith!

A comprehensive understanding of my illness or of its resolution did not derive solely from the revelations through my growing faith. However, within a balanced mindset, renewed and grounded by fervent faith and nurtured in prayer, the remaining answers were clarified.

What's the next step? Where will it lead me? How brightly will His light shine upon me there? I cannot know each answer, but seeking to answer each question makes me trust Him more for each step I take. As we often sing:

> *Each step I take my Savior goes before me,*
> *And with His loving hand He leads the way.*
> *And with each breath I whisper, "I adore Thee;"*
> *O, what joy to walk with Him each day.*
>
> *I trust in God, no matter come what may,*
> *For life eternal is in His hand,*
> *He holds the key that opens up the way,*
> *That will lead me to the Promised Land.*
>
> *Each step I take I know that he will guide me;*
> *To higher ground he ever leads me on.*
> *Until some day the last step will be taken,*
> *Each step I take just leads me closer home.*

Growing in faith, I continue looking for that city. It is sweet to know "each step I take just leads me closer home."

TEN

SO, WHAT NOW?

"Hey, kid, it really is gonna' work out in the end. Really! So, don't worry about it so much! It'll be okay, Paul.

How about we get together and talk it over in about forty years or so? Then you can tell me more of the little stuff I should have noticed along the way. See ya' soon! Yeah, it'll be sooner than you think."

It really is okay. I shouldn't have worried so much. And, the years have passed much sooner than I thought.

Having found higher ground, the view is brighter, calmer and clearer. I am living in a shower of blessings, enjoying a season of refreshing. I am pausing to see from where Jesus brought me to where we stand together today. What a view it is!!

The introspection, the continual striving towards light, the renewal and regeneration, all sound like a lot of work. To anyone making the journey, know it is work. It is also a wonderful journey. And, the work is not nearly as hard as remaining in darkness. The further I pressed on, the lighter the work became. As I found not only light but The Source of Light, the Spirit began its work of regeneration. The Spirit helped carry the load, banished the darkness, and placed me feet on this higher plane.

I wrote previously, "Where is the real victory without the overcoming of trials? The celebration of victory is brighter for having through Christ overcome the darkness." The light does appear brightest when compared to the darkness. So, how does my old self compare with my renewed self?

In darkness, I was controlled by extreme thinking errors,

persistently and dangerously depressed, and socially phobic. I was angry, sometimes manic, and wholly double-minded. The positive roles of my life which I sought to do well – as a husband, father, Christian, and in my work – were each constrained by the label "depressed," and by inordinate and sinful fears.

Now in the Light, I more often thrive within balanced thinking patterns. Light is backing miles away from the emotional edge; hardly remembering the deepest troughs of depression or the sharpest, knife edges of anxiety. Light is the overcoming of social phobias (still a work in progress) by overcoming harshly judgmental assumptions. Light is replacing anger with forgiveness; replacing sarcastic mania with thoughts about "whatever is pure." Light, His Light, is peace.

The transition from my darkness into His Light is voiced in a psalm of Asaph, Psalm 73:21-24.

"When my heart was embittered and I was pierced within, then I was senseless and ignorant; I was like a beast before You. Nevertheless, I am continually with You; You have taken hold of my right hand. With Your counsel You will guide me, and afterward receive me to glory."

The Light also reveals there is work is yet work to be done, for I am still a man tempted by sin and prone to seek my own way. By my nature, I'll struggle against returning to my former mindset in times of trial. There will be adversities which will test my investment in the Truth and my full submission to His will.

The question, "So, what now?" reminds me God is still working. The renewing of the mind is not a once healed, always healed matter. We'd like to think, "Good, I'm all done with that!" However, each one who desires to follow Christ, whether emotionally healthy or imbalanced, needs the continual renewing of the mind. By every sin of our lives, we need continual forgiveness through Christ, and continual healing.

Staking my claim to the higher ground requires knowing how to live within His sustaining Light. This requires knowing what *real* Christianity is. It requires striving towards the goal of having "put on the new self, which is renewed in knowledge in the image of its Creator" (Colossians 3:10).

The desire for higher ground parallels the desire to become more like Christ. Yet, I believe if we reduce becoming more like Christ to our finite perceptions of acting or thinking like Christ, we miss the mark. Reducing Christianity to a set of thinking patterns and life skills reduces God to the limits of man's reasoning.

While I have focused on retraining my mind to draw from a refreshed well of thoughts, real Christianity should not be reduced to a philosophical construct. In one's spiritual infancy, becoming a Christian is a philosophical redirection of one's life. The behavioral constraints expected by the redirection are seen as being Christian. But, Christianity should not remain solely the philosophical template of one who purposes to live for Him.

The philosophies of men, the "systems of principles for the conduct of life" (Webster), negate the leading of Christ, and the indwelling Holy Spirit. Christianity is constrained by being reduced to a set of ethical standards and moral constructs which we follow as law. Rather, our standards ought to grow as fruit of the Holy Spirit living and operating within us.

Because Jesus came not only to save us, but also that we may have life and have it more abundantly, we tend to equate the gospel with being a philosophical means of self-fulfillment and gain. We easily develop a what's-in-it-for-me form of Christianity. When Christ becomes only a self-centered means of abundance - a health, wealth and prosperity gospel - Christianity is debased to philosophy; no higher than mans' wisdom and void of the Spirit.

The philosophical crutch, the constructs and constraints of our actions which we depend upon as a babe in Christ, should be laid aside as we mature in Christ. Maturing Christianity is seeking Christ not only for my redemption, but to walk in a way which will lead others to seek Him for their redemption; well beyond what's-in-it-for-me Christianity.

Defining Christianity as more than philosophy is not a semantic ploy. Christianity is fundamentally a very different premise. Philosophy, born in the finite minds of men, is for lifting up the purposes of men. The call of Christianity, which was born before time from the infinite I AM, is for lifting up God. As Christians we seek to subjugate our wills to His will, trusting His promise that He will lift us up. Christ does the lifting, not us.

Why does the distinction matter? Lifting His call higher than the call of human wisdom reminds me His ways are much higher than mine. It reminds me of His wondrous and awesome powers.

Like a child so full of wonder, we need to preserve a sense of wonder about our God and Savior. But, amid the rampant bombardment of information and entertainments, we are overly intrigued by the things of this world and, sadly, lose our wonder of Him. All which is truly wonderful and uncommon, seemingly becomes commonplace. Thus, it is no surprise those who view their lives darkly lose their wonder of Him. Seeking to remain in His Light, we must like a little child, hold to the wonder of Him and all His ways. We must in awe remember the great I AM who came as flesh, then to die and redeem us from failure. How dare we lose our sense of wonder in Him?

Holding to our childlike wonder, we still must mature. Maturing in Christ is often viewed as thinking more like Christ, or acting more like we think He would act in a particular situation. In recent years we've heard the question, "What would Jesus do?" It sounds fairly high-minded to ask, but in supposing we can absolutely know what Jesus would do, we seek to limit the will and wisdom of God. The question itself sidesteps the fact Jesus did not always perform as expected.

So many times Jesus defied the presumptions of His actions. When James and John sought Jesus to demonstrate His miraculous powers, He did not. When Jesus was sought to condemn the woman caught in adultery, He did not. On trial, when He could have spoken in His own defense, again, He did not. And, when He could have called ten thousand angels to set Him free, He did not.

To be more like Christ is not to suppose to think like Him, but to submit to His leading just as He submitted to His Father's leading. Therefore, Christianity is not a philosophy of self-will for our glory, but is full submission to the Father's will for His glory. And,

SO, WHAT NOW? ➤

real Christianity is submitting to the Word, all of the Word, even the parts we wish weren't there – just as Jesus did. Remember, at the very crux of the gospel, becoming the Perfect Sacrifice for our sins, Jesus prayed, "My Father, if it is possible, let this cup pass from me" (Matthew 26:39). But, then He submitted, even unto death.

I depend upon this definition of real Christianity. It is my submission to Christ just as Christ submitted to His Father. It seems every other picture of Christianity fits within this frame. The definition is simplistic, but it parallels Christ's words. "For I have come down from Heaven, not to do my own will, but the will of him who sent Me" (John 6:38). Jesus left the splendor of Heaven to do His Father's will. My submission costs far less than Christ's.

However, I have not yet fulfilled this definition. As Paul said, "Not that I have already attained it, but forgetting what is behind, I press on toward the goal" (Philippians 3:14). As I consider, "So, what now," the answer lies in striving to become a real Christian according to this definition, not only to remain in the light, but to lead others to the Light.

God has an answer to, "So, what now?" The answer is, "Treat this as a plateau, and remember the journey isn't over. You have not attained all which I have purposed for you, either in this world or for the world to come. Remember, Paul, you've set your goal in My promised glories of Heaven, and we haven't reached the mountain-top. Wait till you see that view!"

Yes, Lord, I do remember my goal.

> *I want to scale the utmost height*
> *And catch a gleam of glory bright;*
> *'til faith has caught the joyful sound*
> *My prayer, my aim is higher ground.*

Akin to the inverted wisdom of God - the last shall be first, the weak will be made strong, and he who gives his life will gain it - I find similar irony in my standing today. Remember my first words: "A life without introspection is a life without a course. A life with too much introspection never pursues its course." I went through a period of not knowing my course. As one who strove to chart every step, once I submitted to Jesus' leading, I did not know my course.

How could I be at ease, a soldier of the cross without His marching orders? But, it was a passing concern. I don't have to know every step. I only have to know my purpose. By committing to the purpose, and not only to the prize, He will direct my steps.

I had to trust, "The secret of the Lord is for those who fear Him. He will make known your course as you reverence His ways" (Psalm 25:14). I understand the design of God's course for my life is not such a mystery, for the Bible tells me plainly, I can know my purpose. At the heart of all I've pursued in the renewing of my mind, the Word tells me the purpose of renewal, and my course.

Personalizing the words in Romans 12:1-2, it would read:

"Therefore, I urge you, Paul, by the mercies of God, to present your body a living and holy sacrifice, acceptable to God, which is your spiritual service to God. And, do not be conformed to this world, but be transformed by the renewing of your mind, so that you may prove what the will of God is, that which is good and acceptable and perfect."

I can know His course for me. I am to use and increase my talents in service to God, pursuing a work which does not contradict His Word, and which glorifies Him. Any work within this standard is acceptable to Him.

There are still days when I chart my own course, largely the result of impatience, thinking as a factor of my middle age, "There's not enough time." Then the Spirit reminds me, "Yes, there is time. God brought you to this time of healing, and He can preserve your days to accomplish what He wills for you." I must remember time is a tool controlled only by the One who existed before time.

Oh my, what a transition this is. Trusting Jesus to direct my steps was foreign to my old mindset. It was only through the Spirit's continual renewing that I have come to trust His continuing "all things for good." The difference is in my decision to "press on toward the goal for the prize of the *upward* call of God in Christ Jesus" (Philippians

3:14). The result is the ripening of fruitful faith. Faith is now a palpable reality in my life. Faith is the real higher ground and the reason the view from this plane is so sweet. Yet, in a balanced mindset, I know every day will not be so.

In the balance of daily experiences, I find the emotionally bright days are often followed by emotionally flat days – "flat" as opposed to dangerously depressed. Those days don't trouble me as in the past. I see them as part of my balanced life, immeasurably better than my old life which was near-always flat, at best. The emotionally flat days remind the seasons of refreshing are seasons; a time to revel in His grace, defend my claim on the higher ground, draw closer to Him, and prepare for whatever life may bring.

Whatever may come, I must be firmly vested in Truth and remember who God is. My thorn in the flesh reminds me of the Source of my faith, and to Whom I will cling, in good times or bad.

> *Life is easy when you're up on the mountain,*
> *And you've got peace of mind like you've never known.*
> *But, things change when you're down in the valley;*
> *Don't lose faith for you're never alone.*
>
> *You talk of faith when you're up on the mountain,*
> *But talk comes so easy when life's at its best.*
> *Now it's down in the valley of trials and temptations;*
> *That's when faith is really put to the test.*
>
> *Oh, the God of the mountains is still God in the valley;*
> *When things go wrong, He'll make them right.*
> *And, the God of the good times is still God in the bad times;*
> *The God of the day is still God in the night.*

These words from the poem, *God of the Mountain,* sustain me, for it is true, faith comes easy when I am on emotionally higher ground. Real faith, sustaining faith, is what sustains when passing through the valleys. Having an attitude of "passing through" is the key; knowing it is only a transition. I refuse to remain in the valley.

I expect the valleys to come will not be so different than the valleys past. The Dark Angel who tempted me in the past will tempt me more so now. The Word assures me the battle for my soul has been won, but the skirmishes will continue. Knowing there is still much to do as I press on to the prize, I recall, "From everyone who has been given much, much will be required" (Luke 12:48). Having been enlightened by His Word and Spirit, and enjoying the light in which I live, I now have a greater responsibility to the Light. Having been delivered out of darkness, I am called to share His light, helping others out of their darkness.

Realizing this responsibility to share, I recall the words of Martin Luther King. "There are millions of people of good will whose voices are yet unheard, whose course is yet unclear, whose courageous acts are yet unseen. These millions are called upon to gird their courage, to speak out, to offer leadership that is needed. History will have to record that the greatest tragedy of this period of social transition, was not the vitriolic words and actions of the bad people, but the appalling silence and indifference of the good people. Our generation will have to repent not only for the words and acts of the children of darkness, but also for the fears and apathy of the children of light."

While his words were a call to bring our nation out of the darkness of racial discrimination, they are also a call to God's people; calling them to courageously bring others into His light. As one who has been given much, I must not resign myself to the appalling silence and indifference, but serve those still struggling in darkness. As a Child of Light, I must give voice to light, beyond the fear and apathy which constrained my past.

As a child chasing horned toads in the pasture behind our house, I often saw a small, spindly-legged bird rise dart from the grass. It ran a short distance, but then fell to one side, with a wing outstretched as if wounded. If I ventured closer, the bird feigned to run again, yet fell again in a more wounded pose.

The bird, a killdeer, was pretending to be injured so a perceived predator would see it as prey, drawing danger away from her brood in a nest nearby. Her instinct to protect her young was amazing! In a moment, without a second thought, the killdeer stood in the gap to protect her brood.

A biblical parallel is in Ezekiel 22:30, where the Lord in His utter disgust with the people of Israel, is about to deliver His wrath against them. Beyond all the abominable sins of the people, their prophets, "whitewash these deeds for them by false visions and lying divinations. They say, "This is what the Sovereign Lord says - when the Lord has not spoken." Yet, the Lord, knowing the full measure of His fiery wrath sought "a man among them who would build up a wall and stand before (Him) *in the gap* on behalf of the land so (He) would not have to destroy it, but (He) found none."

Yes, God was seeking just one to stand in the gap; one who was willing to intercede on behalf of others. Danger was imminent – who would intercede? Perhaps, we do not see ourselves as called to fill a gap which would postpone or prevent the wrath of God. But, like the killdeer, we are called to stand in the gap for others.

Perhaps, my specific call is to stand in the gap for those who are standing way too close to their emotional cliffs. Having found my comfort in the Lord, I must remember "the Father of mercies and God of all comfort, who comforts us in all our affliction so that we will be able to comfort those who are in any affliction with the comfort with which we ourselves are comforted" (II Corinthians 1:3-4). For those who do not trust the Spirit's working, those without comfort, or whose faith has not moved their mountains, I must shine light into their darkness. For those still struggling to find the person to help them, perhaps God wills for me to stand in their gap.

My next step is striving to become "anxious for nothing, but by prayer and supplication with thanksgiving let (my) request known be made known to God" (Philippians 4:6). For one who has long lived as anxious for everything, this next step is a work in progress as I seek to trust the all-sufficiency of Jesus.

It was the anxious-for-everything mindset which held me in darkness. It is the mindset which still, at times, limits my standing in the gap for others, and still shades His fullest light. It is the mindset which must be trumped by believing the words, "For I know the plans I have made for you" (Jeremiah 29:11). I chose Him to resolve my past, I choose Him now to solve the future.

Striving for an anxious-for-nothing mindset is sure reason for each of us, though part of this world, to not live as one of this world. Amid the present tribulations and anxieties of this world, the seemingly senseless wars, the degradation of decency, and economic meltdown, the most obvious physical exercises of many are furrowed brows, neck wrenching, and hand wringing. We are a world anxious for all and fearful of all, while ignoring the call to an infinitely better world.

Yesterday I attended the funeral of a dear friend. Today, another loved one may pass away as I write this sentence. By the number of their years and the experiences in their lives, theirs are similar stories. They are also starkly different, for one lived anxious for nothing; the other lived anxious for everything. One gave every benefit of the doubt; the other doubted every motive of others. One gave selflessly; the other gave by careful measure and the onus of obligation. One ruled with a velvet glove; the other ruled with a boxing glove. The anxious-for-nothing person loved easily; the anxious-for-everything person loved conditionally. Sadly, the latter one believed this is all God intended; despite being His child.

From their lives, I draw meaning from Philippians 4:6, as it affects my ability to love. It seems an anxious-for-everything cannot love in the form as *agape*. Within an anxious mindset, one cannot love without what-is-in-it-for-me conditions. Living as anxious for nothing is rewarded by real peace. It also frees us to love more as Christ loved, in a spirit of selfless humility.

The essential difference in these two lives is one lived contentedly; the other, contentiously. By comparison, I intend to live like the first, to live the words of Psalm 131 – a poignant picture of contentment, freed from striving for gain.

"O, Lord, my heart is not proud, nor my eyes haughty; nor do I indulge myself in great matters, or in things too difficult for me. Surely, My soul is composed and quieted; like a weaned child rests against his mother; my soul is like a weaned child within me."

Past the strivings of this world, how sweet it would be to bear a soul so satisfied and full, longing only to rest in the embracing love of the Savior.

It is like holding my overtired, fitful granddaughter as she struggled so long against taking a nap. She wrestled against my will for her to sleep. She growled and fussed, but in one deep sigh, she relented. She rested contentedly against me in the embrace of love. May I ever do the same in submitting to Jesus, except maybe I have learned not to struggle so long.

The anxious-for-nothing contentedness is only possible by trusting the God of the mountains is also the God of the valleys. It trusts the God who calmed the raging sea, is still God when the sea rages yet again. In Jesus we find our surest anchor in the storms.

Acts 27 tells the story of men who against sound advice decided to set sail against contrary winds. Warned that their trip would certainly be with damage and great loss, they persisted. When the winds briefly suited their purposes, they weighed anchor and sailed. The next day, caught in a violent storm, they could only give in to the angry wind and waves. Fearing they would crash against the rocky shore, they cast four anchors to hold their ship fast. Casting four anchors was not only for safety, but still was a means of seeking their own way. Their purpose was not to save the ship, but to, despite the assurances by God for their ultimate safety, escape the ship.

Facing storms yet to come, I must weigh the four anchors I trust to hold me fast against the waves. It seems three anchors are hoisted and ready – being vested in Truth, giving voice to the Word and prayer, and depending upon the His church. My fourth anchor, a work in progress, will be cast by the fruit of the Spirit.

"The fruit of the Spirit is love, joy, patience, kindness, goodness, faithfulness, gentleness, (and) self-control" (Galatians 5:22). The fruit of the Spirit may seem to be a lighter anchor than the other three, yet the others will not hold without the anchor of Spiritual fruit. Only within the ripening fruit of the Spirit do the other anchors weigh anything. Indeed, my investment in the Truth, and prayer, and the sustaining love of the church are nearly for naught without love, and all the fruit.

The opposite of the spiritual fruit, the deeds of the flesh are as numerous as the sinful ways of man. "Immorality, impurity, sensuality, idolatry, sorcery, enmities, strife, jealousy, outbursts of anger, disputes, dissensions, factions, envying, drunkenness, carousing, and things like these" (Galatians 5:21). Can Truth alone hold me fast against the storms with a heart corrupted by sin? Can prayers bear the strain against a spirit of anger? Will I cherish His church within a fouled spirit of enmities? Certainly not! Spiritually, three anchors will not hold without the fourth. Therefore, the essential answer to "So, what now," is in growing in the fruit of the Spirit.

The anxious-for-nothing mindset demands trusting Him for needs, and trusting His true wisdom to know my needs. It is a mindset well-based on the wise proverb, "Give me neither poverty nor riches; feed me with the food that is my portion, that I may not be full and deny You and say, 'Who is the Lord?' Or, that I may not be in want and steal, and profane the name of God" (Proverbs 30:8-9).

The mindset reminds me of having enough to trust Him as my source, but not so much as to forget He is the source. It is obvious to apply the proverb to financial needs, but its strongest implication for me is in depending on Him to meet my emotional needs; those needs to sustain me against my thorn in the flesh. Trusting His light for a renewed mind, I will pray, "Lord, give me neither all darkness nor all light. Illumine my steps with the light which is my portion, that I may not forget You as the Source of my light." I will add the words by Paul, "For I consider that the sufferings of this present age are not worthy to be compared with the glory that is to be revealed to (me)" (Romans 8:18).

Understanding the balance of my portions, like Paul, I should consider it a light affliction. And, as I remember my Source, may I grow to say, as in the words of Psalm 119, "it was good for me that I was afflicted." God knows when I need more light, or when a measure of darkness will balance my mind.

The goal of developing an anxious-for-nothing mindset is served by remembering, again, the beginning of my healing. It is worthwhile to recall how I became habitually despondent; how depression became my defining modus operandi.

The original intent of my prayer was for release from darkness and relief from burdens. The prayers were for becoming burden free, though that was still an unbalanced goal. Yet, when my mountains had moved, in spiritual euphoria I was blessed by no weight of burdens. I believe the Spirit intended for my spirit to experience an extreme measure of joy and peace. But, life in the extremes, any extreme, is fragile. It is living in balance, with Jesus as the fulcrum which yields a sustained light and a blessed life.

In the vast span of time between Eden and Zion, the life more abundant is not utopian. A blessed life is not euphoric, but one which is balanced in all things – thinking patterns, in words and deeds, in riches and in want, and balanced in the burdens I carry. Whether depressed or not, from the least among us to the greatest, there are burdens which God intends for us to bear.

Continuing healing is a matter of how we bear our burdens, and of which burdens we choose to bear. Living in His sustaining light is accomplished by casting off the burdens we are powerless to change. Living free from the shadows of our mountains derives from understanding which burdens to forfeit, which burdens to endure, and which burdens to take upon ourselves.

Giving up all burdens is not balanced, but is balanced by learning which burdens ought to be endured as a testing of faith which leads to purer faith. That faith will lead us to adopt the burdens we should. We are to, "bear one another's burden, and thereby fulfill the law of Christ" (Galatians 6:1), who so surely has borne and is bearing ours. Bearing some burdens is a light exchange for those we cast aside.

When anxiety builds and darkness looms, it is time for me to test which burdens I am carrying. It is time to be certain I am carrying the burdens which He wills for me. By sorting out the burdens, I return to His sustaining light.

The anxious-for-nothing mindset is established when I am confident of staking my claim on the ground already gained. I must not depend upon Him for the gain, and then revert to my own merits to defend the gain. I must not rest on the yesterday's victory, but depend upon Jesus to meet the foe today. Day by day He supplies to meet the challenge of the day. His manna for yesterday is passed, while His manna for today is new, sufficient and powerful.

What Jesus helped me overcome yesterday, He will help me overcome today. In childlike terms, it is akin to the song about the itsy-bitsy spider which climbed the waterspout. Though having climbed the spout, the gain was not held because more rain always came to wash the spider down the spout again.

Like the spider, I must have through the strengthening of Christ, the innate tenacity and will to climb the spout again. When showers of adversity wash against me, the strength of Jesus will help me climb up again. Victory in reclaiming the higher ground is assured. As the spider relies on the sun to dry up all the rain, I must rely on The Son to lift me again.

The anxious-for-nothing mindset is also challenged by the fear of success. It is counter intuitive that I, wanting to be successful, also have feared it. The anxiety of success is in what may further be expected of me because of success. I have worried, "Will I be up to the next challenge? Will the success last, or will failure come again?" In the cycle of those questions, I revert to the fear of failure, and become anxious for everything.

Sometimes the combined fears of success and failure feel like tightrope walking without a net. Walking in this new mindset is still a foreign experience. Amid its blessings and the assurance of continued blessings from God, sometimes the urge to withdraw is still there.

I am convinced of the blessings in this transformation, but I also believe God does not squander His blessings. His vast storehouse of blessings is for those who continue to seek His will; not cast before swine to trample and wallow upon. I know I can stop this journey at any time. I can balk at the uncertain steps ahead. But, I have now lived long enough in the Light to know if I balk or turn back, I also go back to the ponderous darkness.

There will be days of stress when I may think, "Oh, what am I doing?" I may again be like the Israelites who wondered why God has brought me to this place. Yet, I will remember Jesus came to break my bondage to my old way of living. I will hold to my deliverance from my emotional desert. Returning to that dark desert would be like the dog returning to its vomit. I will not go back!

The cycle of fears is broken by learning not to take myself so seriously, to actually not care quite so much. Yes, you read that right; "to not care quite so much." It requires I understand and really believe that in Christ, failure is not final.

Dan Allender, in his book, *Walking with a Limp,* calls for us to become "carelessly courageous." He defines courage in atypical terms; not as being brave, strong, and invincible. Real courage is being willing to fail, and then trying again.

If we do not feel courageous in the usual sense, we do not think we can step out to serve, or overcome any challenge. Being carelessly courageous means we unload all prideful demands for success, not fearing if anyone sees us fail. The careless courage to let others see us fail encourages them to overcome the fear of failure.

To serve others requires a measure of courage, but we must be careless enough to not fear failure, careless enough to let others see behind our brave mask and shield. Dressed for battle as a soldier of the cross, we must remember the shiny, invincible shield we hold high is not of our making, but is Him. We should remember our victory in Jesus was not based on His strength, pride and appearance. It was based upon His humility, humanity, and submission. Jesus Himself was carelessly courageous; the willing sacrifice for the failures of man.

I want to know more about the accounting of David as having a heart after God's heart. I believe the reason is David, even as a child, was carelessly courageous; careless enough to confront and possibly be slain by Goliath. With careless courage before the giant, David was willing to lay down his life for others, just as Jesus gave His life for all others. David's "heart after God's own heart" is true because of his careless courage to give his life.

A few weeks ago, I was in Barnes and Noble to buy, *Leading with a Limp.* While thumbing through its pages, I heard a gentle, and near-pleading voice ask, "Are you a Christian?" I barely heard the voice and was uncertain of the words I heard.

Setting aside my usual, socially phobic tendency, I turned to see a young man, a high school senior, at the other end of the aisle. He had been reading from a book about the Dalai Lama. As a faithful

Buddhist, the religion in which he was raised, he wrestled with understanding the faith of his Catholic girlfriend. Amid the emotions of first love, he was trying to understand her parents' mindset. While his parents respected his girlfriend's faith, her parents ridiculed his faith. He hoped I could help him understand, even asking me if I thought he should end the relationship.

This was the kind of situation I would not confront before. I would have feigned not to hear and faded around the corner. How could I know what to say to a person whose faith I knew so little? What could I say to settle his mind? But, here was this young man, troubled in spirit and asking, "Are you a Christian?" I had to answer. God deserved my answer.

His questions are those which cannot be answered quickly, but we made a start. His guard was down, and I forced my guard way down, too. I asked him to tell me about his faith, and he was anxious to understand mine. Then I tried to help him deal with the discouragement of her parents.

I received a very rich blessing by stepping out to talk to him and learned again how God can work. Not knowing what to say, but listening with empathy and wanting to share a positive, Christian faith, by the leading of Jesus the words came to me.

Having not yet read the book, I had already stepped out towards becoming carelessly courageous. To help this young man, I had to be careless about what he might think of me. I could not be self-controlling; allowing myself to be vulnerable to failure. I was beginning to learn that "courage is not bravery; it is the commitment to respond to our calling" (Allender).

From the conversation with the young man I was beginning to find a much brighter light. I learned in sharing my darkness to help others find light, or sharing the Truth of the Word, I must become careless. It is inherent within the biblical attitude of service to be willing to set aside my self-worth in order to uphold the infinitely higher worth of God.

Years ago, amid some deeply troubling days, I asked my Dad to share some advice because he had experienced similar darkness. The gist of what he said was simple, "Just take one step at a time; one day at a time." I was disappointed by his answer, thinking, "Oh, come on, Dad, I know you can give me more than that." Yet, now I know he told me much more than I heard. His advice is essential to gaining the anxious-for-nothing mindset.

The anxious-for-nothing mindset requires me to thankful for what I have today; not troubled by what I want for tomorrow. To the coworker who told me I think too much, I admit my anxious-for-everything mindset still too often proves him right. Most anxiety is borne from worrying about tomorrow. But, to be anxious for more than one day at a time denies the promised provision of God for each day. To be anxious for more than today supposes to demand more than I am promised, for tomorrow is promised to no man. Since I cannot forecast those days, their number or their course, anxiety lessens immeasurably if I only focus on one step at a time, on landing squarely the foot which is off the ground at this moment. I do not demand Jesus to direct my steps tomorrow, just the one I am taking right now.

What earthly good is there in worrying about tomorrow? Doing so is counter to the goal I set at the start – setting my hope towards my heavenly home. In living for Christ, whether I live or die is gain. If I am here tomorrow, He will meet every need. If I die, He has already met every need and I will know my life eternal. I am a winner either way!

If I cannot presuppose tomorrow, why should I presuppose its course, or its anxieties? Certainly, we should plan for tomorrow, even dream of tomorrow for the work I do today is the foundation of tomorrow, but as I build the foundation, the step I take today is the one which truly matters. The sum of those steps is, as my Dad says, taking one day at a time.

The essential element in becoming anxious-for-nothing is to pray just as David prayed, "Search me, O God, and know my heart; try me and know my *anxious thoughts*; and see if there be any hurtful way in me, and lead me in the everlasting way" (Psalm 139:23-24). It is still my sinful nature to revive thinking errors, though not so extreme as in the past. By prayer I depend upon the Spirit to reveal those errors, and to lead me back to His better way.

Finally, the sweetest working of God in helping me become anxious for nothing is how He worked through this introspection. As surely as He knows the rapidly declining number of hairs on my head, He knew how to speak to me when I was ready to listen. I see His wisdom to speak in ways He knew I would comprehend and accept. Knowing my passions, I feel He created a parable just for me; speaking in the language of a would-be architect, all about designs and proportions.

From a past obsession of seeking to create the contentment I sought, as if it could be done by designing the perfectly proportioned places to escape, God showed me His better design. Contentment is found by shaping my life according to the perfect proportions of His wise plan. As I press on, the measurements of my contented mind are defined by the length of His mercy, the depth of His grace, and the width of the narrow gate, all built upon the certain foundation of His love.

I previously wrote about my healing beginning in the message by Neale Pryor. The phrase, "failure is not final" was a balm to my broken spirit. The words were the first impression, the first hope I would find solid ground beneath my feet, launching my next steps towards higher ground. While today the view is bright, it is worthwhile to return to Neale's message. There will be failures, and if in those failures the vacuum of depression draws the light from me again, I must remember that in Christ, failure *truly* is not final.

Remembering the scriptural call to remain faithful unto the end, if in the time of failure it is also the time God calls me to that city, shall I fear the judgment? If I have been faithful to the end, there will be no fear, for "the message of the empty tomb is, failure is not final."

While King David was often troubled by his failures, he purposed to build the temple for God. But, it was not within God's plan for David to build the temple. Similarly, as I have purposed to do good for God, if I fail, I will hear the same words God spoke to David. "You did well that you had it in your heart" (I Kings. 8:18).

Those words are a precious assurance of my redemption by the grace of God. As I press on in all good purposes of the Lord, even in failure I should not be anxious, for it is well that I purposed in my heart to do good. The judgment of my life will not be in the number of my steps, or of how many steps were successful. Rather, His Righteous Judgment will assess the direction of my journey and the intent of my heart.

So, what now is the direction of my journey, and what is the intent of my heart? I intend to accept His plan for my life as I learn more of His will. I will seek the continuing renewal of my mind. I will trust God is more than able to meet my needs, answer my prayers, and direct my steps. I will depend upon the Spirit, being my Comforter, my Encourager, and the Guarantor of all which God has promised in that glorious city. I will remain faithful unto the day when Jesus comes to gather all whom God has given Him; to gather all who have held to their calling. I seek the day when Jesus will complete in me the good work He began so long ago. Thus, may I never be found marking time, but always pressing onward, marching onward, and always looking for that city.

IT IS WELL

Moving from darkness into His Light reveals the answers to three persistent questions of life. Who am I? Why am I here? And, where am I going? Finding the answers to all three questions, one will find light. Far better, if all the answers include the names of God and Jesus, one will find The True Light.

I answered the last question first. It is how I started the introspection, by looking outside of myself, and setting my hope in Heaven. Thus, the first answer is, I am going with Jesus to reign in Heaven around the throne of God.

The desire to be reconciled with Him and gain a greater assurance of my faith bore the second answer. Who am I? By the sacrifice of Jesus for my sins, I am a child of God.

As to why I am here – it is, by following the example of Jesus, to glorify God. This must be a continuing answer; one which is the wick and oil of living in Christ's sustaining light. In living to glorify God, the Light will shine brighter over me, and through me.

For anyone who like me has struggled too long in darkness, who is still seeking to find their light, first determine the real questions to ask. Then be assured the answers are found in the all-sufficiency of Jesus and in the Truth in God's Word. Amazingly, when those three answers are known, the other questions of life aren't so daunting.

When I was thirteen years old, attending my Papa's Sunday school class, he taught me his favorite song. *It Is Well With My Soul,* more than any other song, became the tether of my faith in dark times, and is now a song of victory in the good times. It held the words of consolation at his graveside, and holds the words of my fervent expectation of Heaven past my own grave.

When peace like a river attendeth my way,
When sorrows like sea billows roll;
Whatever my lot, Thou hast taught me to say,
It is well; it is well with my soul.

Though Satan should buffet, though trials should come,
Let this blessed assurance control;
That Christ has regarded my helpless estate,
And hath shed His own blood for my soul.

But, Lord, 'tis for Thee, for Thy coming we wait,
The sky, not the grave, is our goal;
Oh, trump of the angel! Oh, voice of the Lord!
Blessed hope, blessed rest of my soul.

And, Lord haste the day when the faith shall be sight,
The clouds be rolled back as a scroll,
The trump shall resound and the Lord shall descend,
Even so – it is well with my soul.

I wish I could sing with Papa today, "It is well; it is well, with my soul." I'd love for him to know the song he taught me is one of the means the Spirit used to work all things for good.

The lightness of spirit which fills my soul today reveals three other questions. Why did I wait so long to believe the God who parted lands from seas, could also part the clouds over me? Why did I not sooner trust my Savior whose power overcame the darkness of the grave, could overcome the darkness of my mind? And, why did I not sooner see all those God worked through to bless my life?

There was my great-grandpa who I've long viewed as the picture of contentment. There was the minister's wife who taught me to love singing. There was my Mom who understood me completely. Surely, I am blessed by my Dad, who still teaches me to step up to the plate, keep my eye on the ball, and just keep swinging. I am blessed by loved ones in whom I see Truth in the flesh. And, my children, who mostly in wonderful times, and in the clearer hindsight of hard times, richly blessed my life. Yes, through each of them, the Spirit has helped sing, "It *is* well; it *is* well with my soul."

As a young boy at the church in Arcadia, Texas, I wish I had known to look northwest across the vacant block toward the corner of 2nd Street. Outside the gray bungalow amid the grove of huge, pecan trees, I may have seen a little girl, first as a toddler sitting in a laundry basket as her Momma took the clothes off the line. Later, I could have seen her helping her Daddy in the garden, or playing with her pet rooster, Scratchy, and feeding him wieners and Coca Cola.

About ten years later, I met her. She grew up and became my wife. In our thirty-five years of marriage, she has been the dearest blessing of this life, a constant, shining light of God, and a constant light to me.

Her life is further proof of the Spirit's working. My desire to press on to higher ground is proof of God's certain answer to prayers. The renewal of my mind and my faith is His answer to my wife's many years of earnest prayers. It is impossible to understand how different our lives may have been without her constant devotion to God and prayer. But, it is easy to understand how our family has been richly blessed by her strength, her graciousness, and her love. God has surely worked His good will through her.

The transitions of life, some predictable and foreseen, and others tragic, were each a means the Spirit could help me to sing, "It is well." Even the introspection which led me out of darkness into His Light, I am confident was the Spirit's working in all things for good. By the Light, I clearly see God's working in my past, His leading in the present, and His promises to sustain me through all transitions of life.

The transitions include the passing of many through whom God worked. The precious great-grandpa who presided over the front porch of the old farmhouse is gone nearly forty years. Mom is gone twenty years. Both of my brothers have died. Indeed, most of the people who gathered for big Sunday dinners at the old farmhouse have died. The rest are scattered by too many transitions to count. Yet, each one is pressing on, still seeking The Light.

The continuing transitions bring me to being the grandpa around the Sunday dinner table. While remembering precious ones from the past, it's time to focus on the precious ones now gathering. As our children bring their families around the table, it's time to help them see the Light. Just as I and those before me have travelled through darkness, they will, too. But, by some word of mine, or more so by the Word of God, may they always strive to move from darkness and into His light.

Seeking His light has been akin to seeking the light of the old farmhouse. When traveling to visit my great grandparents, it was well past dark when we'd arrive. As kids we might sleep part of the way, but as we neared the farm, all wide eyes strained ahead. The house had a single white light mounted high on the front gable, always shining for our arrival. Traveling the noisy and rutted gravel roads over the succession of hills, in the darkness my brothers and I would strain to be the first to see the bright light.

The last valley was the darkest; overshadowed by a thick, canopy of trees. We had to cross a very low and narrow, wood bridge over an oftentimes swollen, rushing creek. But, as we drove up the other side we saw the bright light. Driving through the opened gate and up the long hill, the lone light was the sentinel. Past the darkness, past all the turns and hills in the journey, the light told me, "You've made it home."

Such is the journey and the seeking of His True Light. Through the emotional darkness, past all the hills and valleys, I sought His light. At last, by faith the hills have moved. Now I see His Light, always shining as from the highest gable of my heavenly home. I cherish its glow, for it tells me even now, as the promise of the glorious day sure to come, "Paul, you've made it home."

The old farm is gone now – someone else's lock secures the gate. The old house barely stands in hollow ruins. Surer than sure, all the things of this world will pass away. When I, too, pass away, if I find the gate to Heaven sags just like the old farm gate, and my heavenly home resembles the humble, white farmhouse, I'll still be singing, "I've got a mansion just over the hilltop." I'll be singing in unbridled joy from the front porch of Heaven, there with Jesus and forever His own!

Still, "eye has not seen, nor ear heard, and mind has not imagined what has been wrought for His own," amid the promised glories of Heaven. No tears, no cares, will attend the big family dinners up there. No hurts, no darkness, for the light of Jesus will be there. No prison walls, no imprisoned minds, for our Redeemer frees us there. And, the love of singing which by God's mercy has sustained me this far, will continue there in a new song which will forever more swell and ring! Oh, won't it be wonderful there?

Paul E. Myers

LaVergne, TN USA
07 October 2010
199944LV00002B/50/P